Second Childhood

HYPNO-PLAY THERAPY WITH AGE-REGRESSED ADULTS

Marian Kaplun Shapiro

W • W • NORTON & COMPANY
New York   London

A NORTON PROFESSIONAL BOOK

Copyright © 1988, by Marian Kaplun Shapiro

Published simultaneously in Canada by Penguin Books Canada Ltd.,
2801 John Street, Markham, Ontario L3R 1B4.
Printed in the United States of America.

First Edition

Library of Congress Cataloging-in-Publication Data

Shapiro, Marian Kaplun, 1939–
    Second childhood.

    "A Norton professional book."
    Bibliography: p.
    Includes indexes.
    1. Hypno-play therapy. 2. Hypnotic age regression –
Therapeutic use. I. Title. [DNLM: 1. Hypnosis – in
adulthood. Play Therapy – in adulthood. 3. Psychotherapy – methods. 4. Regression (Psychology) – in
adulthood. WM 450 S529s]
RC499.H94S53 1987   616.89′162   87-20425

ISBN 0-393-70053-4

W. W. Norton & Company, Inc., 500 Fifth Avenue, New York, N.Y. 10110

W. W. Norton & Company Ltd., 37 Great Russell Street, London WC1B 3NU

1 2 3 4 5 6 7 8 9 0

CONTENTS

ACKNOWLEDGMENTS

To thank those who have supported me through the conception and delivery of this book is to give myself the pleasure of reaffirming my love and appreciation for the many people who have given their unique gifts to me. First of all, my family: to my husband, Irwin, who combined his unabashed pride in me with his relentless surgery of unnecessary jargon; to my son Steven, whose expertise with the computer amazed and educated me; to my daughter Nancy, who allowed me to cite her remarkable personal memories as case material; to my daughter-in-law Karen Jo who, planning to enter the field of psychology, braved the terminology and read the manuscript, making suggestions for clarity I gladly incorporated; and to the newest family member, my daughter's fiancé Brian Morin, coming after-the-fact, for his unreserved sense of joy in my success.

I want to make especial note of the personal and professional contributions of Dr. Sandy Rosensweig and Dr. Arnold Abrams. My consultations with them over the years concerning the cases and my personal reactions to them were vital to the work on which this book rests. And I would like to express my gratitude as well to Dr. Gerald Koocher, who, as an experienced author, generously offered his time for consultation. I also thank Dr. Arnold Miller who, despite his own professional commitments, took the time to read and closely edit the first draft of this book with his unique brand of critical acuity and sensitivity. Because of her long friendship with me, Judy Schneider, although lawyer rather than psychologist, marched with determination through the manuscript, making several apt suggestions which improved its logical structure. My warm thanks also goes to Norton editor Susan Barrows for her intelligent, highly skilled contributions to the style and readability of every aspect of this book.

Not to be forgotten are the willing and prompt services of my secretary/research-assistant, Gail Munroe, who literally bore the brunt of carrying books and mountains of Xeroxes to and from my door. Likewise, I thank the reference librarians of the Cary Public Library, who diligently sought and obtained source materials from all over the world. A special category should be constructed for Chris Whalen, computer salesman extraordinaire; from Monday through Saturday he answered my pleas of distress as I mastered the new (and sometimes faulty) technology, making housecalls marked by kindness and patience, and providing loaner equipment during breakdowns. And to Bruce Gregory my appreciation for his Sunday pinch-hitting with the computer. When I feared all was lost, he talked me through a successful resurrection of a recalcitrant backup.

In the most fundamental sense, of course, I owe this book to my patients, whose courage and trust enabled me to discover and develop the ideas and methods presented. I deeply thank them for the permission to share the workings of their minds with others who want to learn from them.

INTRODUCTION

This book represents a journey to a new place. The route we will take is not always the most direct; there is, however, an underlying logic which binds it into its own structure. More like Boston than mid-town Manhattan, the streets meander and curve rather than march ahead in predictable, parallel formation. Unlike Boston, which leaves the stranger signless and stranded, this introduction intends to provide both map and street names. Readers who like to know where they are going will be assured that they are, in fact, passing the designated landmarks en route. Others, who prefer to discover where they are when they arrive, can use this map after the fact, as a review of the trip.

Hypno-play therapy is the deliberate use of play therapy with adults in an age-regressed hypnotic state. Hypnotherapists are familiar with the technique of age regression: The patient, while in trance, returns to a particular earlier age, either spontaneously or at the specific direction of the therapist. While in the age-regressed state, the patient feels as he or she did at the age in question, often reliving events that occurred at that time. When that time is during childhood, the *hypno-play therapist* plays with the patient, as if that patient were a child of that age being brought for therapy.

Hypno-play therapy is based on a simple axiom: If possible, fix the problem where it occurred. Therapists are by nature optimists, believing that even now it is not too late for adults to repair much of the psychological damage they have suffered during their most formative years. Clinical work is based on that assumption, although therapists sometimes make exceptions for certain serious conditions; at the least, for example, we usually restrain our enthusiasm about the possibility of fundamental change for patients with characterological disorders.

Hypno-play therapy not only addresses the repair of the discrete tear in the fabric of early development – the single trauma, let us say – but also and importantly addresses the development of seriously impaired, repeatedly traumatized, and/or chronically deprived people. Through the medium of play, such patients are given a second chance at childhood with the therapist as deputy parent. Because such work is done in trance state, the intensity of the relationship between patient and therapist becomes magnified in both directions. Through the process of introjection, patients incorporate the new, nurturant experience so that it eventually becomes available to them as a Kohutian selfobject throughout the rest of their lives.

This book is divided into two sections: The first, *A Context for Hypno-Play Therapy*, places the technique of hypno-play therapy within the theoretical background from which it emerges. Readers are asked to take a developmental and interactional view of human beings, and to consider such terms as regression, introjection, transference, and countertransference from that perspective.

Section II addresses the actual *Practice of Hypno-Play Therapy*. After first defining our terms in Chapter 4, we look at the use of this treatment for neuroses and characterological disorders in Chapters 5, 6, and 7; we then spend Chapters 8 and 9 detailing the methods of induction and hypno-play therapy itself. Chapter 10 consists of a discussion of clinical and environmental problems encountered in the practice of hypno-play therapy. Since now the reader will know the purpose and method of this technique, we discuss in Chapters 11 and 12 how to select appropriate patients for whom it might be of benefit. Chapter 12 is the period at the end of the sentence, the resting place at which we stop. The reader is encouraged to continue on to further uncharted territory, where both new answers and new questions await.

The principles that will be presented in Section II are those which represent the closest fit to my observations, and from which my approach to hypnotherapy therefore evolves. Taken separately, these ideas are not unique. Many theorists have laid ground before me: In attempting to credit these authors, I have doubtless omitted many who have come to similar conclusions independently. Surely, many readers will hear their own thoughts on the following pages, as well as the echoes of those of their colleagues and predecessors. This book, however, will simply present the ideas as mine; in no way, however, is there any implication that they are mine alone.

The case examples cited to illustrate the theory and process have not been cleansed of inconsistencies or of difficulties experienced by the therapist. They are intended to be provocative rather than to serve as standards for slavish imitation. Yet, some imitation by the novice can, at first, serve a useful purpose, for until there are established workshops in the technique of hypno-play therapy, the prospect of working in this mode might well evoke the practitioner's anxiety and avoidance rather than the spirit of informed adventure. Thus, I encourage the interpolation of the reading of Section II with sessions of practice. First, the reader can begin such sessions by role-playing the transcripts themselves with colleagues. Reaching a comfort level with the text, the reader can then move to the rehearsal of his or her own cases, past or present, and to the anticipation of difficulties that might arise, and results that might accrue, in order to animate this section at every opportunity.

Hypno-play therapy is not a miraculous cure-all. It is, simply, a direct and forceful way to reach the child in the adult, the child whom we, as therapists to adults, often talk *about* but rarely *meet*. If we can meet the child, we can work with the child. In that way the child can grow up and become a whole and authentic adult.

I

A CONTEXT FOR HYPNO-PLAY THERAPY

1

THE EVOLUTION OF
A HYPNO-PLAY THERAPIST

I am going up in an elevator. The building is the seven-
story apartment house where I grew up. There is a man in
the elevator, a colleague, dressed professionally, whom I
do not identify. The elevator goes to the roof, beyond the
point where, in fact, it went in real life. We get out. I walk
to the edge of the building and look over. I see huge building machinery – cranes, derricks – knocking down and
erecting other structures, crashing their wrecking balls
with impressively loud sounds. I am in awe of the enormi-
ty of what these machines are doing. I look behind me to
see if my colleague is coming to join me. He is standing by
the elevator door. I wish he would come and keep me company.

I dreamed this dream in 1981, four years before my conscious decision to write this book. At the time, I was working with five or six patients whose hours were spent totally,
or almost totally, in a regressed state. My colleagues and
consultants were supportive of this work, but, like the man
in the dream, they stayed at a distance from the edge at
which I felt myself to be standing. Worlds were being destroyed and created in front of my eyes, impinging on my
every sense, and company out there was not available. I had
taken the elevator beyond the conventional limit – and up to
that point I had a companion – but out on the edge of that
roof was too far! Perhaps it was even too far for me. The
reader will scarcely miss the male imagery which pervades

the construction site. Moreover, that side of me that works with theory, the rational, cognitive, orderly side, who often emerges as the male counterpart in my dreams, seemed to be taking an observer position, when I yearned for a closer partnership. My dream made it clear that for me, as a woman, hypnotherapy felt like new and earth-shaking territory. In reality I did have little female company; the representation of women in the professional hypnotherapy societies, such as the American Society of Clinical Hypnosis, reaches barely 15% of the membership even today, and from visual observation I would guess that it is far less than that at the advanced level.

Over the years since that dream I have moved in the direction of creating a constituency to stand on the edge with me. To this end I have attended meetings, given workshops and talks, and written papers. Most important, I have set aside several clinical hours for teaching and supervision of graduate students and experienced practitioners seeking training around their work with people in the age-regressed mode. Teaching is, of course, the best way to learn a subject thoroughly. As with all teaching, the requirements of effectively conveying the material to others forced me to greater clarity and organization of the subject matter. But best, these students and supervisees, ever inquiring and persistent, made sure that I was challenged and pressed to develop a sound theoretical base for the practice of hypno-play therapy.

Additionally, during these years of relatively solo excursions into the theory and practice of hypno-play therapy, I did, in fact, make contact with an occasional colleague who had made unpublished forays into the same or similar thickets. Emily Rupert, for example, a social worker and clinical teacher of transactional analysis, ran weekend therapy "marathons" in which sessions were held in a room dubbed the "playpen." This setting, resplendent with pillows, stuffed animals and baby bottles, when teamed with the group process, supported and sometimes actively encouraged the participants' regression to preschool ages amidst a controlled holding environment (for further description, see Levin, 1974).

Hypnotic "reparenting," a structured attempt to correct developmental distortions through "change-history imagery" (Stricherz, 1986) also bears some similarity to the work to be described here.

But such innovative approaches have been few and fringe rather than "growing edge" in the community, for among traditional psychodynamic therapists the very idea of promoting regression is viewed negatively; at best such practice is seen as risky, at worst irresponsible and unethical. Having respect for caution and for the importance of solid theoretically-based practice, I felt uncomfortable without a community of my colleagues with whom to stand.

Among hypnotherapists there was more interest, as most hypnotherapists had included age regression among their armamentarium of hypnotic techniques – but usually in isolated instances rather than as a treatment method in and of itself. Arnold Miller, for example, director of the Language and Cognitive Development Center in Boston, Massachusetts, a clinical psychologist known mostly for his work with autistic children, instinctively combined his more recent training in hypnosis with his knowledge of play therapy, occasionally making use of children's games during age regression (Miller, 1986). Katz (1985) also reported on his "little" play work with adults: "By learning to experience the world through play, one learns to play with fear, to play with anxiety, and to transform experience so that it becomes more positive" (p. 311). For the most part, these psychotherapists were using hypnosis congruently with its limitations, as set out by Spiegel et al. (1981): "Hypnosis itself is not a treatment modality. Rather, hypnosis is a method of disciplined concentration which can be used adjunctively with a primary treatment strategy" (p. 239).

In contrast to Spiegel, I see the principal use of regressive hypnosis as therapy itself. Hence, hypnosis, as for Gardner and Olness (1981) in their work with children, is differentiated from hypnotherapy: Hypnotherapy, forming the skeleton of a longer-term procedure, becomes the principal treatment more than an adjunct to treatment. Through the broad application of the hypnotic state, patients otherwise un-reachable, or reachable only after many years, can be touched in places they had hidden so thoroughly that they appeared to be imbedded in stone, if existent at all. By ex-panding the use of hypnosis with such people, I have found that when age regression is teamed with the use of play therapy, not only can such places be contacted and extended, but empty spaces are filled in and nurtured as well. Then the more conventional psychoanalytic model, with its golden cornerstones of interpretation and insight, can be followed to good effect.

Think of the sense that this proposition makes! In the following case, a typical use of hypno-play therapy, namely, play therapy in the age-regressed state, is offered, illustrat-ing its function for an adult for whom therapy as a child would have been beneficial. In the example below, Larry, age 30, was treated with age regression, from which the follow-ing details emerged.

LARRY: UNRESOLVED GRIEF

When he is four, Larry's one-year-old sister dies in an acci-dent. On the day of the death, no one in the family pays attention to him; he is sent to a neighbor's during the funer-al. Afterwards, his pregnant mother retreats to her bed, emerging pale and uncommunicative. Father returns to work. Shortly thereafter, a baby appears. No one mentions the dead sister; her toys and clothes disappear. One day, the little boy finds a picture of his sister in the attic and brings it downstairs. Father snatches it away from him.

Larry becomes quieter and quieter; when I meet him as an adult, he speaks so softly as to be barely audible. He tells me of a time in his late teens when he stopped going to school, remaining in bed all day, drifting in and out of sleep, barely eating, neglecting to wash or shave, smoking pot and drink-ing instead of eating. He remembers that no one in the fami-ly commented on his behavior; catching sight of his rachitic appearance in the mirror he finally became frightened, and began to eat again, returning to school voluntarily and deciding to study hard and go to college. His job now: a social worker with refugees from Southeast Asia.

Had a therapist seen Larry at age four or five, the issue of unresolved grief would have been unmistakable. Some combination of play therapy and family work would have been the obvious treatments of choice, were the family not resistant to such efforts. But in many ways this patient was still four or five years old, desperately seeking to resolve those issues through his employment, where he spent extensive time with families in which loss and grief – and especially the loss of children – was a pervasive theme. Therefore, the mode of approaching the problem *where it really was* called for the use of play therapy with the patient in the regressed state of hypermnesia, where he could experience the intensity of the traumatic event, as he had been unable to do given the environmental conditions at the time. For this patient there was play with dolls and puppets acting out the funeral; later, we threw snowballs at trees in the yard until verbal anger could replace silent physical expression.

In fact, of course, the traumatic event had not been limited to the death, but in a broader sense included all of those aspects of life from that day on, in which Larry learned to hide his feelings, to literally shut up, to let himself waste away in what he described as an attempt to demonstrate – since talking was not allowed – that he was dying.

WHY HYPNO-PLAY THERAPY?

Before being formally trained in hypnosis, I practiced in a relatively conventional psychodynamic mode – one-to-one "talking cure" therapy, with an occasional collateral visit with spouse or family. I had, as I have still, a view of the human being as an amazingly resilient creature, elastic beyond belief, capable of immense courage. In that cycle of positive expectations leading to positive results, a satisfying percentage of my patients "got better"; their symptoms remitted, their lives improved. That is still true—so what is the difference?

Basically, there are two points on which I rest my case for the deliberate application of play therapy through age regression during the hypnotic state: (1) With characterologically disturbed patients (in current terminology, personality disorders), the changes made possible by hypno-play therapy are more than symptomatic—they are fundamental. The saying goes that you cannot make a plant grow by pulling on its leaves. The use of hypno-play therapy allows the patient's new behavior to emerge out of a grounded, well-fertilized sense of self, which all of us know is foundational and meant to be based in very early childhood. Thus the new behavior feels relatively natural to the patient—expanding what Winnicott (1958a) identifies as the "starting place" of what he terms the "true self" rather than alien to it. (2) As my dream implies, such renovation is often large-scale and fast, where the foundation has been made sound. Erika Fromm (1980) states that "the main motivation for most of us who become hypnoanalysts has been the desire to help our patients solve their conflicts faster than is possible in psychoanalysis or in psychoanalytically oriented psychotherapy in the waking state. Often what can be done in three years of psychoanalysis can be done in three months or even three hours of hypnoanalysis; and without a loss of depth, or a loss of permanency of change" (p. 426). The building is knocked down; the new edifice is constructed. The details of the remodeling job are up to the owner, and can take a long time to be completed, but the basic work is done and the environment is radically altered. Where the foundation is weak or virtually nonexistent, there is finally potential for real, solidly based gains. This is the revolutionary potential of hypno-play therapy.

Many cases, such as that of Larry, resolve smoothly, without serious complications. But such rapid demolition and reconstruction are not without hazard. These are violent words for violent acts. Angyal (1982), in fact, uses these very terms in his discussion of depth-oriented treatment. As he

puts it, "When his neurosis is threatened the person feels
that everything is falling to pieces, that he is about to dive
into nothing, that he is dying. Parting with neurosis feels
like parting with life" (p. 240). He notes that this process can
be dramatic or subtle, but that, in fact, the shift from neurosis to health is in some sense a total one. As in the famous
rival-form reversal illusion of the vase and the profile, all the
elements of both representations are present in each, but,
depending on the orientation of figure to ground, the picture
is different—entirely different. Much goes into the preparation for the shift that seems to occur as if by magic; much
pain and desperation precede the miraculous blink of the eye.
The patient has invested everything in the view of the world
as he or she has lived it. Between the woman's profile and the
vase—two radically different world views—lies a menacing
cavern: the patient, experiencing "the bankruptcy of the neurosis . . . as his own total bankruptcy," "feels hopeless, utterly ignorant of life and how to conduct it" (Angyal, p. 225). No
wonder that there is a risk of suicidal despair.

Because of this very real life-threatening potential for suicidal despair, creating a safe place for the patient is mandatory, especially when working with more seriously disturbed
people. Building a positive transference within a Winnicottian holding environment through hypno-play therapy oriented at an early developmental level seems a promising
route. Fromm (1980) exhorts the therapist, "Give to the patient—do not take away!" (p. 426). Yet, during the demolition
phase, the patient feels as though all of the methods by
which life has been made supportable have been destroyed.
The patient must continue to live while the new ways of life
are taking hold. Interventions from many angles must be
considered, medication and/or protective housing included.
One possibility is the introduction of a series of (hypnotic)
structured visualizations to facilitate the repair of the developmental deficits (Brown and Fromm, 1986, pp. 259–260);
thus, the patient can return to some earlier place experienced as safe. This idea represents a repudiation of what I
have often termed the "iodine theory": the more it hurts, the

better it is for you. One cannot want a healthy life without
the feeling of health as a reference point; one cannot even
believe in health, much less withstand excruciating misery
for the hope of it, without even a moment of knowing it as
personal truth. From that search for a combination of new
soil for new growth and the immediate sustenance for life in
the here and now, the healing possibilities of play therapy for
adults in hypnosis naturally emerge.

2

AGE REGRESSION

Perhaps the reader will accuse me of indulging in a how-many-angels-can-dance-on-the-head-of-a-pin exercise in this chapter. Slogging through various definitions of such familiar terms as "regression," "decompensation," "compensation," and "reconstitution" will likely lead to loss of patience with what may feel like endless quibbling over hair-splitting minutiae. That the reader and author must agree to speak from the same vocabulary is a common rationale for the stress on precise terminology; were that the only reason, one definition for each term could be offered and stipulated, and we could be done with it. But I hold the strong conviction that language influences action in subtle, unconscious ways, that human behavior is limited by words whose meanings have become infused with silent approbation, with affects such as fear and disapproval. Eventually, these affects, operating invisibly underground, restrict our vision and our degree of freedom as practitioners.

Hence, this chapter asks the reader to confront all assumptions about these concepts, which are fundamental to the work of deliberately induced age-regression. I urge each of you to talk back, argue, confront the ideas offered here and those you have accepted as givens, to upset your equilibrium with questions rather than to assuage it with answers.

THE MAJORITY VIEW OF REGRESSION AND
RELATED CONCEPTS

Our society is unforgiving in its stance toward childishness among those past whatever age has been designated as
adulthood. Starting with the Biblical injunction to "put
away childish things," adults are exhorted, in impatient
tones, to "grow up," to "stop behaving like a child." Even
children taunt and tease their peers at any sign of childish
vulnerability. The awful threat of being called a "baby"
pushes the nine-year old girl to surrender her attachment to
her "blankie" and the seven-year-old boy to quickly assert,
"I'm fine!" after a painful tumble.

Professionals, not too differently, are also likely to eschew
a return to or display of childishness in their adult patients.
For psychotherapists outside of the practice of hypnotherapy, the word *regression* most frequently calls up associations
of serious psychopathology—the red alert, especially for
those who work primarily in an outpatient milieu. Text after
text marries regression to "pathogenesis" and "acting-out,"
with frequent reference to ensuing psychiatric hospitaliza-
tions; Masterson (1985), for example, links "regressing in
acting-out" in both text and index.

Freud (see Strachey, 1966) considered (Breuer's) "topo-
graphical" regression, "temporal" (or "developmental") regression, and "formal" regression to be theoretically distinct, although he recognized that all are "one at bottom and occur
together as a rule; for what is older in time is more primitive
in form and in physical topography lies nearer to the perceptual end" (p. 548). Freud's (1911–13) interest in regression
was directed towards the location of the "fixation point" to
which the libido flows, that pregenital "previous stage . . . to
which the function may regress if the subject falls ill through
some external disturbance" (p. 318; also see Freud, 1925, p.
268).

This exact point was of particular interest to Freud (1925)
in his theoretical presumption that its "localization . . . is
what determines the *choice of neurosis*, that is, the form in

which the subsequent illness makes its appearance" (p. 36, italics his). Given that "neurotics are anchored somewhere in their past," Freud (1916–17) postulated that this "somewhere" is located at a period in which the libido felt satisfied, in which the person felt happy. Now suffering from the unpleasantness of a symptom which has resulted from a regression to that period, the patient comes for treatment (pp. 365–366). And as long as the patient remains ill, he or she inevitably returns to that fixation point, at which the libidinal energy has been retained, until it is resolved.

Thus, the process of regression is conventionally seen as purposive, simply, as an "unconscious defense mechanism in which a person undergoes a partial or total return to earlier patterns of adaptation" (Kaplan and Sadock, 1985, p. 80). As is usual, however, the union with abnormality gains momentum with the text's next line: "Regression is observed in many psychiatric conditions, particularly schizophrenia" (p. 80). Even more vividly, the *Longman Dictionary* describes the "reversion to immature behavior" as a "revival of earlier reactions such as weeping, pouting, thumb-sucking, or temper tantrums. . . . In chronic schizophrenia patients sometimes regress to a completely infantile level where they have to be washed, dressed, and fed, and in some cases assume a fetal position" (p. 628). Thus regression becomes the sick process of a sick mind.

Now it is obvious that the word regression is, of itself, devoid of fearsome qualities. Webster's Third New International Dictionary identifies its origins in the Latin *regressus*, first defining it neutrally as "the act or privilege of going or coming back." As a second thought appears the now more conventional, medical definition of regression as "a previous and esp. worse or more primitive state or condition," with further reference to "progressive decline of a manifestation of a disease."

This incessant barrage of negativity has its effect on us as practitioners. Professionals or not, we too are storehouses of the overtones with which our unconscious is laden – the words and nonverbal associations of our daily interactions on this earth. Bad. Sick. Our intellect may subscribe to Winnicott's (1958d) paean to artistic expression as he proclaims that "we are poor indeed if we are only sane" (p. 150n); nevertheless, we worry about our own regressive behaviors and feel uneasy with regression in our patients.

Anna Freud (1963), reminding us that the child's "occasional returns to more infantile behavior," such as in falling asleep, can be "taken as a normal sign" (p. 132), proclaims that regressions "serve adaptation as well as defense and/or help to preserve the state of normality" (p. 137), that regression is "a normal process" of "two-way traffic" (p. 139). This statement does not reassure us, however. Like Anna Freud, we believe, at best, that "this beneficent aspect of regression refers only to those instances where the process is temporary and spontaneously reversible"; when not, it "becomes a pathogenic agent" (pp. 136–7).

Kris's (1952) "regression in the service of the ego" is a horse of a different color. For healthy "artists," such regression, sometimes termed "adaptive regression" (Scagnelli-Jobsis, 1982, p. 41), can be a positive experience, leading to the possibility of what Kris calls "a combination of the most daring intellectual activity with the experience of passive receptiveness." This achievement, however, presupposes the "integrative functions of the ego" having reached a level of "self-regulated regression" (p. 318). But what a risk! As Anna Freud (1963) puts it, it is "almost impossible" to determine whether a regression will be reversible. Who would be willing, then, to gamble, to take the risk of becoming a murderer of one's patient's mind?

Linked in the same way with the negative view of deliberately induced regression is *psychological decompensation*, usually defined as something like "the appearance or exacerbation of a mental disorder due to failure of defense mechanisms" (Stedman's Medical Dictionary, p. 366). The *Longman Dictionary* details the results of decompensation, which is described as "a gradual or abrupt breakdown in the individual's psychological defenses, resulting in neurotic symptoms, such as depression or anxiety, or in psychotic symptoms, such as thought disorder (delusions, hallucinations, feelings of unreality" (p. 204). Meissner (1978), without defining the term, simply refers to his patients' decompensation as a "break"; next thing we know, they are in the hospital. When the term is used medically, as in the failure of normal functioning of an organ such as the heart, the mood is certainly grim.

Since decompensation is a flight from *compensation*, is compensation a positive state of events? Compensation can be viewed either as conscious or unconscious. But since compensation in itself is, as the *Stedman's Dictionary* puts it, "a mechanism by which the individual tries to make up for fancied or real deficiencies" (p. 304), recompensation (when referred to at all, usually termed *reconstitution*) is simply a return to a defense, rather than to a state of health. So we have a double message: Leave the defense mechanism alone, but conduct psychotherapy nevertheless.

Imagine, then, this scene: You are presenting a case to some respectable, supervisory individual or group, reporting a session in which your patient, let us say a successful accountant, has "decompensated" and behaved in a "regressed" manner, reaching for your shiny paperweight, rubbing it on his skin, touching it to his mouth, smiling dreamily, and saying, "pretty, pretty." What response do you expect from the group? As presenting therapist, how do you feel? Confident? Curious? Excited? Or are you anxious? Guilty? Penitent? Defensive? My guess is that one of the latter adjectives would be more accurate. As Balint (1979) puts it, most of our kindest colleagues would consider a patient's regressive behaviors "an important factor in pathogenesis, and . . . a formidable form of resistance," as "undesirable symptoms caused by a questionable technique, or as indications of such disturbance in the patient as to make the prognosis doubtful" (p. 153). Even experienced contemporary writers who eschew rigid dogma warn, as does Weiner (1986) that "the treatment techniques that fostered greater regression [have] more potential for doing damage . . . " (p. 105).

Of course I am making a generalization. We must remember the exceptional work with schizophrenic patients of the pioneers in the era before antipsychotic medications came into use (see Barnes and Berke, 1971; Sechehaye, 1951). And there are doubtless numerous unpublished and slightly published practitioners (some, perhaps now reading this book) who have pressed ahead through their work with their regressed patients, finding value rather than blanket dismay at that condition. These are therapists who, on their own, learning from their contact with their patients, came upon what Winnicott (1958c) described as follows:

> One has to include in one's theory of the development of a human being the idea that it is normal and healthy for the individual to be able to defend the self against specific environmental failure by a *freezing of the failure situation*. Along with this goes an unconscious assumption (which can become a conscious hope) that opportunity will occur at a later date for a renewed experience in which the failure situation will be able to be unfrozen and reexperienced, with the individual in a regressed state, in an environment that is making adequate adaptation. The theory is here being put forward of regression as part of a healing process, in fact, a normal phenomenon that can properly be studied in the healthy person. (p. 281)

As Winnicott accurately states earlier in this paper, it was a living case, not theory, that taught him most, that made him "different from what [he] was before." It "called on everything that I possess as a human being, as a psychoanalyst, and as a pediatrician. I have had to make personal growth in the course of this treatment which was painful and which I would gladly have avoided" (1958c, p. 280).

What one needs when undertaking deliberately regressive psychotherapy is – to use an overworked term – support in one's professional life. One needs nondogmatic, nonjudgmental supervisory consultation with interested, curious colleagues. As in the other aspects of training, one also needs theoretical underpinning and instruction. Encouraging the former, this book will attempt the latter goals, accompanying the reader to that perilous and exciting edge of the roof.

REGRESSION AS VIEWED BY HYPNOTHERAPISTS

As the reader has doubtless gathered, regression is viewed without horror by hypnotherapists. In fact, it is considered one of the hallmarks of trance state. Most hypnotherapists would probably agree with Gill and Brenman (1959) in their opinion that "every psychotherapeutic situation is to some extent an invitation to the patient to regress; that such regression usually takes place in greater or lesser amounts in all psychotherapies where the patient is reached at all; and that when hypnosis is used in psychotherapy we can observe this phenomenon more closely because it is greatly intensified" (p. 328). The capacities for auditory, visual, tactile and olfactory hallucinations, as well as evidence of dissociation, are standard items on scales of hypnotic susceptibility (Hilgard, 1965); note that these are identified as *capacities* rather than as *symptoms of mental illness*.

For hypnotherapists regression is a process, which, in careful hands, can be titrated according to the needs and developmental structural integrity of the subject. In age regression, the patient is most often induced in just such a way, with a limited, clear goal, bounded by time, circumstance, and contract: For example the patient dreams in a session intending that a particular issue be illuminated, or a patient preparing for dental surgery is directed to a happy, peaceful time in the past or in fantasy. With reasonable attention to patient screening (see Chapter 11), these procedures are benign.

Less frequently, but more to the point of this book, *hypnosis is used to work through specific traumatic incidents, to complete and integrate stages in which development has been inadequate or problematic, and/or to initiate or further characterological reconstruction.* Most important, as Gill and Brenman (1943) point out, such regression, including revivification, differs from actual reliving of the original time by the fact that it "takes place in the frame of the *present* personality structure . . . " (p. 167, italics mine).

Erik Erikson (1968) rather dramatically speaks of the "radical search for the rock-bottom . . . , the only firm foundation for a renewed progression" (p. 212). In a sense age-regression is the search for that firm foundation that hypno-play therapy attempts to create. Rock-bottom is usually someplace in childhood, and play is what we instinctively do with children. It is the language that they hear and the language that we instinctively speak with them. Despite the physical differences between adult and child, in an important way, the regressed adult patient *is* little. We must learn to recognize that and to be with that child.

Age regression is one of the conventional techniques of hypnotherapy — if there is such a thing as a conventional technique in this field. In the age-regressed state the patient experiences what Hilgard (1977) terms "a genuine *retrogression* . . . in which there is a return, through memory, fantasy, and hallucination, to something actually experienced at an earlier time in the person's life" (p. 44, italics his). Such a time can be chosen deliberately either by the adult patient or, rarely, by the therapist. More often, the focus evolves through the patient's unconscious, linking past and present via feelings in what Watkins (1971) calls the "affect bridge" (p. 22). Moreover, memories are often mood-dependent; as Bower (1981) has illustrated, "Events learned in one psychic state can be remembered better when one is put back into the same state one was in during the original experience" (p. 130). A psychobiological approach to the understanding of that process is brilliantly investigated by Rossi (1986).

Indeed, the recent literature, for example Nachman and Stern (1984), indicates that "in early infancy, when affective functioning is thought to be relatively more essential for adaptation, affect can be re-evoked by cues even after long delays. This finding suggests the presence of a memory storage system, including affects, that are recallable by cue very early in infancy, long before the emergence of a language or symbol-based semantic recall system" (p. 100). If recallable during infancy, why not recallable later on? We need to accept that it is more than likely that our patients are capable of recalling, and may in fact recall, such early affects from the vantage point of the memory of a similar affect at an older age.

During age regression patients may "see" themselves eidetically on an imagined (hallucinated) screen, remaining detached from the feelings of that scene, observers of their own life. Or, more theatrically, the scene may be revivified, that is, patients may feel themselves to be the age to which they have regressed, speaking and behaving as if they were there. There may be great catharses of traumatic events previously fully or partially forgotten: "Simple" personal and war-related post-traumatic stress syndrome (Brown and Fromm, 1986) is often treated successfully in this manner. In fact, one wonders if hypnosis, utilizing dissociation in induction, might be especially powerful because of its same-state similarity to the spontaneous dissociation evoked by sudden trauma.

It is worth noting that therapists including the use of abreaction in their work are in agreement that, when followed by interpretation and integration into the adult personality, abreaction is, as Watkins (1980) avers, "a valid therapeutic maneuver" that should be retained and further studied "within the therapeutic armamentarium of a successful therapist" (p. 102). In the rare case of an unexpected multiple personality, the particular personality that emerges during hypnotic regression can be handled in an age-appropriate way, helping him or her to fill out the developmental arrest and to integrate with the other personalities (see, for example, Fagan and McMahon, 1984; Sach and Braun, 1986). To employ hypnosis would be to intensify the work and to heighten the process of internalization.

APPLICATIONS OF AGE REGRESSION

The results of severe trauma—war, child abuse, molestation, natural disaster—are familiar to all of us in our work as psychotherapists. The revivification of such horrific events is hair-raising, shocking, even to the observer. More frequently, however, the general outpatient psychotherapist will encounter revivification of ordinary events that were traumatic *for the child*—the injury of a pet, a betrayal of trust by a parent, a disappointment in the birth of a sibling. The themes of these occurrences can often be lost in the seeming insignificance of the memories. One must keep in mind that in all of these, however, there is an important point that we must not undervalue: Something about the event was taboo. Something could not be talked about. Something remained incomplete, and, feeling dangerous and overwhelming to the little ego, became repressed and therefore unassimilated to the adult with adult reality-testing capacities.

ELLEN: LIFE AS TRAUMATIC CONTEXT

Ellen, as a little girl living in abject rural poverty, observed that when her parents could not afford to feed the work horse, the father shot it. She concluded that such would be the fate of the children who, being brutalized regularly for their lack of productivity, were surely less valuable than the horse. Hypnotherapy revealed the following scene that, in itself, seemed an ordinary lingual confusion common to all children, scarcely traumatic. In school one day the teacher lined up the first-graders for yearly photographs. When Ellen waited outside the room, seeing no one come out (as the children before her had exited by another door), she "knew" she was going to be "shot," the word the teacher had used. For her, this benign event became an anticipated execution—about which she would never feel free to talk to her parents, of whom she was in mortal terror. Chronologically in her forties, this patient, in many ways a competent, professional woman, remained six years old or younger, hyper-vigilant, a fragile bird perched precariously on the end of a branch, ready to take flight at the slightest breeze.

A case like this will not yield to memory or even catharsis. Much rebuilding is called for. This event from Ellen's life would earn no tabloid headline; rather, her life itself was a traumatic context. Here the therapist can make the greatest contribution in revising the context. First, the patient must remember, then reexperience, then understand. After that it becomes possible to work through and heal.

General memory facilitation is another common use for the deliberate induction of regression. Memory, censored by amnesia both limited and broad in scope, is, as a by-product of repression, the very substance of every psychotherapy. But retrieval and enhancement of memory of places, events, and such are controversial (see Loftus and Loftus, 1980, for an excellent discussion).

Hypnotherapists specializing in forensics are appropriate-ly concerned about the trust with which the public views the information emanating from subjects in trance. Their testi-mony may influence the verdict of a trial, for example, and, if viewed as somehow above question, can become lethal. It has been reliably demonstrated that: (1) Deliberate falsifica-tion of trance can successfully fool a therapist, for, as Orne (1979) elegantly put it, "As a rule, the average hotel credit manager is considerably more adept at recognizing decep-tion than we are" (p. 334). (2) Falsehoods can be introduced by the therapist – inadvertently or otherwise (see, for exam-ple, Lamb, 1985) – or can be manufactured by the patient while in trance. The recitation of these "pseudo-memories" which the patient has confabulated in a mixture of fact and fantasy will be thoroughly convincing to any naive observer, and even to the patient, whose "memory" has gained "subjec-tive conviction" (Orne, 1966) through, perhaps, "importa-tion" and "assimilation" serving the well-known human need to fill in gaps and make sense of the universe (Paul, 1959, p.

55). And (3) accurate memory can be enhanced through hypnosis (see, for example, Williams, 1985).

Lucky are we, however. As nonforensic hypnotherapists, we need not worry about veridicality. Without concern for detail, which some authors believe is likely flawed, our focus can rest on the emotional aperture that the hypnotic state provides or enlarges (see, for example, Nash et al. 1986). We can entertain as many doubts about accuracy as our temperament and the situation warrant—as long as we can join the patient in feeling. As Winnicott (1958b) noted, in writing about birth memories and birth trauma, *"While disbelieving the details described as memories, I found myself prepared to believe in the accompanying affect"* (p. 179, italics his).

This is not to say that we should automatically doubt the authenticity of what we are hearing. Recently, it has been proposed that "hypnosis may improve memory only when the learning situation is traumatic," since repression and/or the impact of the event may have caused what seemed to be "less salient details" to be set aside (Baker and Patrick, 1987, p. 178). It may well be appropriate to encourage the patient to discuss the remembered event with other people who might be in a position to supply details; to check municipal records; to take the part of sleuth in the service of a grounding based on integrity. More often than not, the memory, especially if the hypnotherapist has taken care to remain objective, holds many nuggets of factual, verifiable truth. No matter how repugnant the details, this corroboration offers a sense of relief to the patient. Thus, as hypnotherapists, we need to be sensitive to all the shades of meaning in our patients' productions be they narratives, T.A.T. stories, free associations, fantasies or dreams.

VICTOR: COMPULSIVE GAMBLING

Victor, a 37-year-old programmer, brutally abused by his mother as a child, had been unable to stop a pattern of compulsive gambling and violent outbursts that was putting his marriage in jeopardy. In trance he regressed to the

age of five. Partially opening his eyes, he saw himself playing
alone in a room, sorting baseball cards. He reported feeling
"lonely." His mother, cleaning in the kitchen, did not want his
company. None of his 12 siblings was home. I held up a
generic magic wand (a clear plastic tube), saying, "If you had
three wishes, what would they be?" He thought carefully. "A
Tonka truck," he said, brightening a little. "And what would
be your second wish?" He looked down. "I wish my daddy
would play with me." Aware that daddy worked two jobs, I
knew that such a wish did not seem likely to be fulfilled.
"And what is your third wish?" Tears appeared in the "five-
year old"'s eyes. "I wish I had a new mother."

I do not know if my patient had baseball cards or if the
room in which he saw himself was arranged as he reported it.
Trial-ready evidence was irrelevant. What I do know is that
Victor was able to begin to talk about the repressed, guilt-
infused feelings of disappointment in his previously idealized father, hatred and wishes for revenge that he felt towards his mother, and a general yearning for attention. All
of these were reflected in his compulsive, destructive behavior.

Through play therapy Victor can explore these feelings,
expressing them through the behaviors and "voices" of puppets, in painting and clay, in music, with water, and with
construction equipment. Patients like Victor can safely express their rage through these media until it finds its verbal,
adult expression towards the original objects. Gradually patients like Victor can learn to love and hate the same person
and can come to terms with the coexistence of the power of
these feelings in a lasting and nonsadistic relationship.

Balint (1979) puts it well:

> [The therapist must] help the patient to develop a
> primitive relationship in the analytic situation corre-
> sponding to his compulsive pattern and maintain it
> in undisturbed peace till he can discover the possibil-
> ity of new forms of object relations, experience them,
> and experiment with them. Since the basic fault, as

long as it is active, determines the forms of object relations available to any individual, a necessary task of the treatment is to inactivate the basic fault by creating conditions in which it can heal. To achieve this, the patient must be allowed to regress either to the setting, that is, to the particular form of object relationship which caused the original deficiency state, or even to some stage before it. . . . Only after that can the patient "begin anew," that is develop new patterns of object relations to replace those given up. (p. 166)

In some sense this philosophy is true to basic psychoanalytic practice; regression is encouraged through the supine position of the patient and the relatively "blank screen" position of the analyst, with the incumbent sensory deprivation. But analysis is most appropriate for those whose egos have developed beyond the rudimentary stage. Kohutian techniques stretch the patient pool of psychoanalysis by aiming at the development of a selfobject which would grow from the finger-in-the-dike model to the evolution of the patient's own self: After a two-stage "defense analysis," including the "unfolding of the transference," would follow the revolutionary third step, the "opening of a path of empathy between self and selfobject . . . [which] permanently takes the place of the formerly repressed or split-off archaic narcissistic relationship . . ." (Kohut, 1984, pp. 65-66). In the model of hypno-play therapy the characterologically immature person has the opportunity to introject the caring presence of a supportive, nurturant adult and then to develop that introjection into the selfobject towards which Kohut aspires.

3

THE HYPNOTIC
RELATIONSHIP

HYPNOTHERAPY: A BI-DIRECTIONAL, INTERACTIVE MODEL

Sometimes it seems that hypnotic trance (synonymously termed *trance state* or sometimes simply *hypnosis*) defies definition. Some attempts consist of a list of behaviors of the patient (or "subject"); hypnosis is a one-man (and, following the Svengali model, it usually *is* a man) show, marked by, as Freud (1905) described it, "an attitude of . . . subjection on the part of one person towards another . . ." (p. 296). Very often, especially since the 1960s and the prevalence of mind-altering substances, hypnosis is identified as "an altered state of consciousness" whose function is "regression in the service of the ego along with increased access to the unconscious" (Fromm, 1980, p. 430).

Hilgard's (1965, pp. 1–10) itemized definitional menu of hypnosis is typical:

(1) "Subsidence of the planning function" (loss of initiative). Behavior is felt to be involuntary or spontaneous.
(2) "Redistribution of attention" (selective attention and selective inattention).
(3) "Availability of visual memories from the past, and heightened ability for fantasy-production" (as in age regression).

25

(4) "Reduction in reality testing and a tolerance for persistent reality distortion" (Orne's [1959] "trance logic," for example, termed "a tolerance of logical inconsistencies" by Watkins [1984, p. 87]).

(5) "Increased suggestibility."

(6) "Role behavior" (role-playing).

(7) "Amnesia for what transpired within the hypnotic state."

Transference and countertransference in
hypnotherapy: necessary, powerful, and
problematic

The standardized definitions of hypnosis do not, however, tell the whole story: There are *two* people involved in hypnotherapy (which is one reason why auto-hypnosis is a subject unto itself, not here considered). Gill and Brenman (1959) accurately assert that hypnosis, which they describe as "a state of altered ego-functioning," is a "transference phenomenon." Freud (1913) identified "an attitude of *rapport*" as virtually synonymous with "an effective transference," which is "the first aim of the treatment" (p. 139, italics his); elsewhere (1921, p. 58), in relation to hypnosis, he refers to "transference onto (the hypnotist)," a one-way view.

In this classical approach to transference, the analyst is seen as the stand-in for the earlier, more important real object, now become the internal object; *pathological* responses emanating from the patient's history are repeated with the therapist. The wider view sets transference within the context of normality; typical of such an outlook is that of Loewald (1960), who avers that "Any 'real relationship' involves transfer of unconscious imagines (*sic*) to present-day objects." He observes that once the transference neurosis is resolved and the relationship between patient and therapist becomes more real, even the new object relationship with the therapist "is not devoid of transference . . ." (p. 32). In this orientation, transference becomes "a universal characteristic of relationships" and is "an essential determinant of all psychic reality" (Michels, 1985, pp. 13–19, pp. 18–19).

Certainly there is nothing to keep us from looking at transference from *both* angles: From one, transference is defined as the specific and awesomely powerful relationship between patient and therapist in which the components of the patient's early inner life take on new energy as they convey themselves onto the person of the therapist, with all the distortions born of earlier experiences, some preverbal, many unavailable to conscious evaluation and control. It is this aspect of transference that is even further potentiated and exaggerated by hypnotherapy. When discussing the influence of hypnosis, the word "primal" keeps coming up: From Stone (1961) we hear about the "general latent craving for an omnipotent parent" which "can produce the profound physiologic alterations of hypnosis" pressing, by its "primitive power" towards the "primal transference" (p. 71). Angyal (1982) similarly describes transference in the hypnotic relationship as taking on an "all-inclusive, totalistic character" in which the therapist is experienced as the *"primal* parent" who is "almost one's whole world." (p. 121, italics his). Accepting that limited-angle aspect of transference, we also need not reject the second broader attitude that says that *all* aspects of our lives are felt in the context of our past; surely it is an accepted fact of life that we learn – both consciously and unconsciously – from experience! Thus, even the best-analyzed therapist will have both conscious and unconscious responses to the patient. These we call countertransference, again, both limited and broad.

The second, more systems-oriented attitude to hypnosis and the transference engendered in the hypnotic relationship is represented by the view of rapport as a two-way street. Here the relationship is sometimes a blatantly maternal one, in which, as Kubie and Margolin (1944) explain, there is a "dissolution of Ego boundaries [which] creates a psychological state which is analogous to that brief period in early infancy in which the mother's breast in the mouth of the infant is psychologically a part of that infant. . . ." In trance "the hypnotist becomes partially engulfed within him . . ." (pp. 612 and 618).

Following that orientation, but taking a more interactional systems view, Laing (1985) eloquently links therapist and patient as "conspirators," which, as he points out, means people who breathe together, people such as a mother and baby, or two lovers. Here we have, then, Winnicott's (1958e) "nursing couple" (p. 99). Even more vividly, Kestenberg (1978) sees the psychological space between people as almost a physical mutual incursion that he names "transsensus." Extending from that view, we should attend to Benedek's (1959) thesis of the co-development of parent and child in their interactional behavior, in her important article detailing the "spiral of transaction" (p. 405).

In the same vein, Erickson approaches the hypnotic relationship from a cybernetic position; that is, he sees the therapist and patient as simultaneously influencing the reactions of the other, through a feedback mechanism: Hypnosis, he says, is "a vital relationship in one person, stimulated by the warmth of another" (Zeig, 1985, p. 63), slyly avoiding identifying which person is which. As Matthews (1985) puts it, "Who is hypnotizing whom is a matter of perspective" (p. 50).

Thus, finally, we can define hypnosis as *a transactional relationship involving two people, each affecting the other, each functioning in an altered ego state.* To repeat: *Both therapist and patient are in an altered ego state.* And in that state all of the above changes are occurring.

Gill and Brenman (1959) refer to "a few reports where the hypnotist speaks of feeling 'somewhat dreamy and removed'" during induction and of being especially reactive to trance productions, which, they also note, are intrinsically more affect-laden anyway (p. 99). It is my experience with perhaps as many as 50 colleagues and students that the hypnotherapist is *always* working in a state of light trance, both with patients and even in practice sessions with peers; this impression is validated by four empirical studies reviewed by Diamond (1980). In what Diamond elsewhere

(1984) calls the "tango," both the transference and the countertransference are heightened in hypnosis, when compared to the usual work done by the therapist. This state of events, while causing many technical problems, some quite serious in nature (see Chapter 10), is not all negative. As the patient's associations loosen, so must the therapist's, if the therapist is to keep the patient company. Thus, as Diamond eloquently puts it, "the hypnotherapist must oftentimes feel and experience the patient's unconscious affect and images within himself, courageously tolerating the pain and uncertainty, while managing to remain strong, consistent, and 'good enough' to provide sufficient comfort and direction for the patient to go on with the healing journey" (1984, p. 9).

Indeed, as Kohut (1959) asserts, introspection and empathy (which he links in the descriptive term, "vicarious introspection") "are the essential constituents of psychoanalytic fact finding" (pp. 463–5). Among supposedly nonhypnotic analysts, there are those such as Loewald (1960) who recognize that, when the patient is functioning on a more "primitive" level, the analyst's "communication with the other person then tends to approximate the kind of deep mutual empathy which we see in the mother-child relationship" (p. 21). Coming from Benedek's (1959) contention that there is actually a "structural change" in the parent as well as in the child (p. 392), Brown (1984) notes that "the patient actually participates actively in creating in the analyst what I call the 'developmentally appropriate parental response'" which "*emerges within* the therapist" and that "subtle perceptual cues of this developmentally appropriate attitude play an essential role in setting the analytic scene" (pp. 106, 108, italics hers). The self psychology school stresses the "mild and controlled" state of regression which the therapist will permit in himself so as to allow "aspects of the analysand to be experienced as part of the analyst's self and become available for introspective examination" (Wolf, 1979, p. 455). In real life the mother spoonfeeding her baby opens her own mouth spontaneously; in the hypnotherapeutic regression, the therapist opens his or her mouth—and considers the meaning of having done so.

Such co-regression is, at the least, problematic. It can be frightening indeed in a relationship with a psychotic patient, whose projections are felt as an impingement on the therapist's own identity in the resulting fusion (Boyer, 1979, p. 353). All therapists—hypnotherapists or not—must be free to follow their patients, to "co-hate" and to "co-lust," as H. H. Watkins (1980, p. 103) puts it. The "healthy split" recommended by Racker (1968, p. 62) cannot be employed in the presence of the patient, or the patient, sensitive to the extreme, will feel abandoned. As has been noted, many "hypnotists recognize in themselves an important need, however well or poorly disguised, to control other human beings [through] overt energetic tyranny . . . [or by] an all-giving position which seeks to control by engendering dependence" (Gill and Brenman, p. 93). It is said that such hypnotists often abandon the technique, feeling intolerable anxiety in its practice. In fact, rather than the infantile sense of ultimate, magical power which attracts/repels prospective hypnotherapists, the successful hypnotherapist must let go of that conscious control long enough to move with the patient in the patient's unconscious life—while simultaneously retaining the responsible caretaking faculty. A fine line indeed!

The therapist as good mother

Of course what we are talking about is the mothering function. As Kubie and Margolin noted as long ago as 1944, "Ontogenetically the hypnotic process can be viewed as a phenomenon of regression in that it approaches the sensorimotor state of an infant in the first weeks of life" (p. 611). Who is boss, mother or baby? Any parent knows all too well that the baby, with its incessant demands and total physical dependency, rules the household; schedules quickly adjust to baby's needs. The good mother feels deprived—and she is—of sleep, adult activities, comfort. Best is the situation in which the mother gets some of her own satisfaction from the relationship, while being mature enough to realize that the baby's needs take preeminence for the time being. To do this she must have had most of her basic needs attended to at the appropriate developmental time. This ideal mother recognizes the need for and can attend to her current deprived state, seeking help and support elsewhere as needed, and still enjoying particular aspects of the alliance with her child. So too for the hypnotherapists who, in that illusory state of "mental health" towards which we all struggle, undeniably receives some "satisfaction he thinks he otherwise could not attain" in the interpersonal relationship with the patient, but who avoids the perils of what Lindner (1960) terms the "shared neurosis."

Most hazardous to the mother, as well as to the hypnotherapist working with major hypnotic regressive work, are not the technical complexities, some of which will be detailed in Chapter 10. Rather, I suspect that it is the regressive pull, the yearning for that "fusional communion" (McDougall, 1979, p. 291), that time in which wishes became gratifications, seemingly out of thin air, in which we were cared for with no effort of our own, in which our needs were met as if by magic, in which we were loved for no reason, when we took without guilt, lived only in the moment when, as Silverman and Weinberger (1985) put it, "Mommy and I [were] one."

Thus, that fantasy, particular and general to us all, of what we got and what we did not get lures us, teasing our vulnerabilities in the business of hypnotherapy. We can easily be seduced by the yearning for what Freud (1930) termed oceanic bliss: "a feeling as of something limitless, unbounded," of "an indissoluble bond, of being one with the external world as a whole" (p. 65), what Fenichel (1945) called "magical communion" (p. 63) – the urge to merge with humanity, to connect to eternity. As one patient put it, this "longing for the boundaryless place" can be overwhelmingly intense.

As the patient feels that longing, which, to some extent, becomes satisfied in trance, such feelings are reactivated for the therapist whose patient, at the level of the archaic mirror transference, "experiences the analyst as a part of the patient, a part which is totally merged into the patient's self-experience" (Wolf, 1979, p. 448). This is more than what Racker (1968, p. 134) calls "concordant identification." The therapist feels uncomfortable with this sensation of having been vaporized, but additionally suffers the "narcissistic resonances" (Wolf, p. 451), never completely eradicated, of yearnings to reverse the positions between the nurturant therapist and the satisfied patient.

Of course it is, then, the boundary issue at which we come to rest, the basic I/you dance, the fundamental need-fear dilemma with which humans come into the world. Born still attached, the baby has spent nine prenatal months aware in some undefined way of the maternal environment. Suddenly, the cord linking baby and mother is severed. Baby sucks on mother's body, connected once again, then put down. Picked up, held, rocked, left, talked to, fed, ignored . . . in such a way the ego emerges, grasping the *I*-ness of the self, the *not-I-ness* and, eventually, the *you-ness* of the other, the space between with its rudimentary sense of anxiety and loss. All of us have come from that remarkable and mysterious process. Somehow, when things go well, baby feels the world as a Winnicottian "holding environment"; it is part of what Benedek calls "the relationship of confidence." This basic trust in the world becomes that which makes the hazardous business of being alive tolerable.

Our introduction to survival thus is everyone's history and, to some extent, the foundation of the work of every course of psychotherapy. When, as therapists, we make it possible for others to explore such issues as "unthinkable anxiety" in their primitive origins, we indeed must be comfortable with our own development in this area. As Diamond (1984) puts it, citing supporting work by Kline and Orne, "The clinical hypnotist, like his/her patient, must also 'let go' and risk an intense, interpersonal relationship. . . . Entering into such intensified empathic bonds while remaining capable of separateness and therapeutic objectivity is no mean feat" (p. 6). In the land of bi-directional boundary permeability, one treads carefully. On the one hand, if we allow our boundaries to loosen too far, psychotherapy will turn into the therapist's self-gratification; on the other, if we insist upon strict boundary maintenance we will become counterphobically rigid and our patients will – rightly – feel abandoned.

INTROJECTION: THE PRIMARY OPERATIONAL MECHANISM IN HYPNOTHERAPY

> I was in some town, an ugly town, with tall wire fences and cars lined up all around, and houses that were like factories. I was on the second floor, just waiting. Somehow we got word that something had happened. I went out on the street aware of the danger, to see. . . . Some power source was being piped in. . . . I began to walk around looking for my car.
>
> – Excerpt from Elaine's dream

The fundamental psychic mechanism in hypnosis is introjection. This is so to some extent even in the most mechanical of hypnotic inductions, such as a routinized "stop smoking" program, but it is overwhelmingly true and important in reconstructive hypnotherapy. Gill and Brenman's (1959) patient says, ". . . all the time when I go into hypnosis, I feel that I take you down with me . . . that you go down inside of me *with* me. . . ." (p. 87, italics theirs). Through the patient's experiences with a satisfactory good external object – the "power source" – new good internal objects can form and develop.

We start from the Kleinian position that in a normal developmental order of things introjection may be the first mechanism of psychological growth. At first we see the primitive, "cannabilistic" stage that Freud (1905, p. 198) termed *incorporation*, in which "sexual activity has not yet been separated from the ingestion of food." As baby observes mother's face and manner, baby absorbs the look, the tone, the touch as reflections of itself and, we theorize, begins to construct the self-image – lovable, disgusting, whatever – on which its personality will be founded. Teamed as it is with the era of breast-feeding, that is "to that brief period in early infancy in which the mother's breast in the mouth of the infant is psychologically a part of that infant" (Kubie & Margolin, 1944, p. 612), and with the first glimpses of separation into I and Not-I (Winnicott, 1965d), introjection is an oral mechanism: The power source is being "piped in" to a barren, vaguely dangerous environment (further discussion of Elaine's case follows in Chapter 10). In introjection it is as if baby were eating the feelings and attitudes of its immediate world, that food becoming part of its body, undifferentiated from it. Here, truly, is primary process.

The following case example will likely sound familiar to most readers – vague, chronic depression, resistant to medication or conventional psychodynamic therapy. Many other methods of treatment could have been attempted: cognitive, rational-emotive, expressive – there is a host of possibilities. Here the approach is based on the importance of replacing a negative introjection with a new, positive, selfobject:

MARLENE: BORN INTO GRIEF

Marlene, a 39-year old nurse, is marking time as a clerk. She tells me that she has been depressed all her life. Though neat and clean, she is dressed in no-color clothes: toneless browns, washed-out beiges. Her skin and hair are sallow, and she speaks in a monotone. She says that she intends to kill herself when she turns 40. Two courses of individual psychotherapy and one psychodynamic long-term group have not changed her outlook on life. Trials of antidepressants have produced only side-effects. She has no incentive to live.

Marlene's history, on the surface, seems unremarkable: only child in a stable, middle-class family, no early losses, no abuse, an unexceptional academic background. The feeling I come away with is one of silent grief. We talk – we get nowhere. Her current life is almost eventless. She feels depressed, and yet she functions within the normal parameters, eating and sleeping without disturbance, moving at an average pace, thinking clearly, without bouts of anxiety or fits of weeping. Here is where I begin to think about failure at the level of introjection and inquire about her family's emotional state during her infancy. She does not know, but agrees, with much hesitation, to address this question to her aunt, being afraid to raise the issue directly with her mother. Her resistance cues me to note the presence of some taboo about the subject or about the possibility of talking about anything vital (with double meaning to that word) in the immediate family.

The information seems too predictable to be believable — but it is true. There was another baby, a boy, born dead, for which my patient, conceived almost immediately after the first death, was to be the replacement. We can hypothesize that the behavior of both parents, still grieving for the first loss, reflected both that loss and *their* grieving selves. Being unable to cathect positively — or perhaps at all — with their new daughter, they became her introject. Absorbing that introject, Marlene later expressed that introject through her depressive projections: I am valueless, unlovable. She saw herself in the mirror of her mother's face, a face which, in its incomplete grief, had to reject her. She should have been dead — and she was going to act that out.

In such a case, to replace the introject of the bad object with a good one seems the most logical direction. Hypnotic trance, especially trance making deliberate use of age regression, exploits the loosening of more mature defenses and encourages the opening of avenues towards earlier developmental levels at which re-introjections can take place. For, as Smith (1981) states, "In the case of psychopathologies whose developmental arrests occur earlier [than at the oedipal level], the 'transference' term does not apply in the classical sense. Here the relation to the hypnotist takes on characteristics of a *real object* as opposed to a transference object" (p. 59, italics his).

Hypno-play therapists take the Kleinian position that, in Kernberg's words, "The introjection of good experiences gives rise to good internal objects, which constitute basic stimuli for ego growth" (1985). Elaine's dream shows us her inner world of sterile ugliness, replete with inhibition (tall wire fences) and lack of affective, empathic relationships (houses that were like factories). Marlene's world was as drab and colorless as her clothes. Through the presence of what we hope to be the therapist's healthy ego, with its well-developed but flexible sense of boundaries, the undeveloped or damaged ego of the patient can, as Masterson (1976, p. 340), put it, ally with "the therapist's healthy ego . . . as a result of the patient's having internalized the therapist as a positive object," eventuating in the development of a new object relations unit.

Recall that we are dealing with the period that precedes the formation of boundaries, the period in which there is the faint beginning of a suspicion of the existence of bodily separateness, perhaps as early as the first one or two months of life. This process of reintegration is more than what hypnotherapists have called "ego-strengthening" – this is an *ego reformation*, the second stage (or, in the words of Elaine, the "second floor") of the work in which we are involved. In her dreams, Elaine has arrived at the point at which she can look for her car (the toddler, perhaps, who has learned how to "walk around"), but she wakens before locating it. Through play as well as through the arduous period of verbal working-through, the formation of a strong and healthy foundation for developmental growth can take place. She will then be able to find her car and to drive it to a destination of her own choice.

One final postscript. Transference and introjection owe their potency to their origin in the natural history of the human being. We do not manipulate these phenomena like technical tools – rather, they emerge and empower the therapy from beginning to end. As such, we owe these so-called theories more than mere respect: We owe them our profound thanks for their contributions to the success of this remarkable process of psychotherapy.

II

THE PRACTICE OF HYPNO-PLAY THERAPY

4

WHAT IS
HYPNO-PLAY THERAPY?

In Abbie Farwell Brown's children's book, *The Lonesomest Doll*, the Queen, herself a little girl whose parents
"had died when she was a wee baby," meets up with her
servant's child, Nichette, who has discovered the Queen's
storeroom of untouched toys. Nichette, the daughter of loving parents, is shocked at the Queen's neglect of her dolls.

> "How would you like to be left day after day alone,
> with no one to love and kiss you?"
> The Queen's face turned still pinker.
> "I have no one to love me," she said.
> Nichette stared. A Queen, and no one to love her!
> This was very strange. "Why don't you play with
> your dollie, then?" she demanded. "I have no broth-
> ers nor sisters, but I have my dolls, and I play with
> them in the garden all day long."
> The Queen looked puzzled.
> "Play?" she said. "How do you play with a doll? I
> don't know how to play."

In and of itself, doing play therapy with adults is not a
revolutionary idea. As Anna Freud (1964, pp. 61–62) noted:
"If an adult neurotic came to your consulting room to ask for
treatment, and on closer examination, proved as impulsive,
as undeveloped intellectually, and as deeply dependent on

his environment as are my child patients, you would probably say, 'Freudian analysis is a fine method, but it is not
designed for such people.' And you would treat that patient
by a mixed method, giving him as much pure analysis as he
can stand and for the rest children's analysis – because, ow-
ing to his infantile nature, he would merit nothing better."
From conversation with my colleagues, I know that this idea
has occurred to many, such as Brown and Fromm (1986),
who recommend "a playful therapeutic atmosphere" for patients who have missed the playful aspect of childhood (p.
283); some therapists of my acquaintance have acted upon
their instincts to do play therapy with their adult patients in
isolated instances. Additionally, we are familiar with the expressive therapies, which incorporate elements of play in
their approaches to adults.

Hypno-play therapy goes one step further: it is the use of
play through *therapy* with adults in an *age-regressed* hypnotic state. The Queen is still a child; she will learn from
Nichette. Were she an adult, however, teaching her how to
play would be a difficult task, for which hypno-play therapy
would be appropriate. By this technique we would gain access to the child state in which play therapy will be most
beneficial. To appreciate the synergy that makes this technique especially effective, we need to look at and attempt to
define each of its components separately.

COMPLICATIONS OF DEFINING
THE MEANING OF PLAY

It seems almost ridiculous to have to ask the question:
What is play? We all know, of course: As adults, we play
music, tennis, ball; we play with ideas; we allow play, or
slack, in an electrical cord; at considerable cost we attend a
play. We know what we mean when we tell our children to go
outside and play. And, importantly, if they are normal children, they too know what to do, although they have never
struggled with the problem of defining the commonalities
among the many variables in their play activities.

Webster's Third New International Dictionary devotes a full three columns to its attempts to list all possible uses of the word 'play.' What comfort in the ease of allowing "play" to be dismissed as "an overflow of surplus energy," as Alexander once viewed it (French, 1961). Rather, the truth seems to be that play is, in Erikson's (1964) phrase, a "borderline phenomenon" which "in its own playful way, . . . tries to elude definition" (p. 4).

Not only does it try—it succeeds! But, nevertheless, academicians trained in the scientific method are rightly uncomfortable with a nonscientific, non-academic approach, in which a definition cannot be honed and agreed upon. I am reminded of Humpty Dumpty's position in *Through the Looking-Glass* (Carroll, 1946, p. 94):

"When *I* use a word," Humpty Dumpty said, in rather a scornful tone, "it means just what I choose it to mean—neither more nor less."

"The question is," said Alice, "whether you *can* make words mean so many things."

"The question is," said Humpty Dumpty, "which is to be master—that's all."

Thus, theorists, hoping to be master, argue from every conceivable position: intrinsic vs. extrinsic motives, biological imprinting, historical recapitulation, psychoanalytic development. From almost any podium can emerge yet another heroic angle of attack on the problem (See, for example, the extensive summaries offered by M. J. Ellis, 1973). Others try to define by contrast: We say, blithely, "All work and no play makes Jack a dull boy." By this aphorism we contrast and isolate work and play, rather than accepting the more complex model of the continuum with its large area of overlap. In that way, of course, the search for simplicity leads us to imply that work is that which is onerous and likely obligatory, while play is pleasurable and voluntary. Admitting, with Gottfried (1985), that "play is easier to recognize and observe than to define" (p. xvii), writers, including Gottfried, nevertheless set out to do just that, codifying play into subtypes: exploratory play; functional play; constructive play; object-oriented play; unstructured play; solitary, parallel, and social play; imaginative play; and games with rules. The list is sometimes shortened to consist of functional play; constructive play (preschool); dramatic play (beginning during preschool years); and games with rules (after age six or seven, continuing into adulthood) (Rubin, 1985, p. 89).

How, then, shall we look at the meaning of play in the particular context of hypno-play therapy? Garvey (1977) wisely concludes that "the central notion (of play) seems clear enough, but the fringes of the concept are fuzzy." Following that axiom and abandoning the search for an airtight definition, I will concentrate only on that central notion, the often-cited inherent qualities of play, namely, the capacity for freedom, creativity, and flexibility. Spontaneity and experimentation are core to this outlook (for discussion, see Kagan, 1981, p. 82f). As Winnicott (1986) puts it, "creativity is inherent in playing, and perhaps not to be found elsewhere" (p. 64). Creativity is the watchword of play — to imagine, to try out, to suspend reality, or to expand it in any direction. In psychoanalytic terms, we can say that the ego is allowed to grow by drawing from the id so that the synthesis of the two, to be refined by superego functions, moves the person towards a higher level of development.

In short, as I use the term here, the capacity to play is very closely aligned with the quality of vitality that makes one fully alive. As Beckwith (1985) observes, parents "have a central role . . . not only as caregivers but as playmates" (p. 157). In fact, the parent is the child's very "first play companion and tutor. . . . " It is the parent who "stimulates, facilitates, and models play for the child" (Irwin, 1963, p. 167). The Queen, you recall, was an orphan since infancy. *In loco parentis*, the play therapist takes on this parental role when working to develop the sense of play in a child/adult who was deprived of these experiences.

PLAY THERAPY

Play therapy is, simply, the use of play by a therapist with a child patient, for one and/or two overall purposes: the working-through of a troubling emotional experience; and the development of the child through a stage that has not been successfully negotiated. "Maladaptive behavior," often cited as the rationale for the choice of play therapy, is not required (Phillips, 1985, p. 752). In the strictly psychoanalytic approach pioneered by Melanie Klein (1975), the child's play activity is viewed as symbolic, and, like the adult's use of free association, is interpreted by the analyst. A less orthodox approach following the work of Anna Freud (1964, p. 35) instructs the play therapist to see only *some* of the child's play behavior as symbolic, recommending selective interpretation. The therapist may control the direction of the session, guiding the play towards the areas he or she feels to be important or, like Axline (1947), take a nondirective approach, waiting for the relevant material to emerge from the child, allowing the child "to experience growth under the most favorable conditions," and utilizing the child's "natural medium for self-expression" (p. 16).

AGE REGRESSION

The basic purpose of age regression is the revivification of past experience. The infinitive *to revivify* (from the Latin *revivificare*) is not quite identical with *to revive* (from *revivere*), although revivification is often used as if the two words were synonymous. To revive is, according to Webster's Third New International Dictionary, "to live again; to return to consciousness or life; to recover life, vigor, or strength; to become reanimated or reinvigorated; to become active, operative, valid or flourishing again; to restore to consciousness or life." Additional subdefinitions include "to raise from languor, depression, or discouragement; to raise from a state of neglect or disuse; to renew in the mind or memory, bring to recollection, recall attention to." All of these phrases ("live again," "return to," "recover," etc.) infer that the original memory had been alive, and that reviving it creates a *restoration* of the original state which had once been experienced. I will use the infinitive *to revivify* instead, preferring its precise meaning: "to impart *new* life to" (italics mine). By doing so I assert that the original event was not, in fact, fully experienced at the original time. In bringing it to the forefront of memory, the person has the opportunity to experience fully what was cut off and not experienced at some level during the original event in question.

It is, of course, understood that the patient's body has undergone considerable change since the initial experience. Even if regression could, as Erickson avers, "rearrange the patterns and neurological processes" (1986, p. 51), regression does not ablate subsequent change. Physical growth (both external and internal) and cognitive development have modified the person's capabilities for understanding and response. Although there have been reports that some infant reflexes, such as the plantar, the sucking, and the grasping reflex, can occur in adults age-regressed to infancy (see Brown and Fromm, 1986, p. 32), an excellent experiment by Silverman and Retzlaff (1966) confirms "the Piagetian claim that structural intellectual changes during development preclude a reversal of stage sequence," and that hypnotic age regression "is not a literal regression to childhood" (pp. 9, 200). In some way, then, despite the most vivid appearance of the events of childhood and their age-appropriate behaviors, such as childlike vocabulary, drawings, and so forth, the adult is ever an adult; the patient's observing ego (see, for example, Hilgard, 1977) remains on the scene, watching from its corner observation post. However, this fact need not deter us; in fact, some benefits accrue. For, as Gill and Brenman (1943, p. 167) noted, since hypnotically induced "reliving . . . takes place in the frame of the present personality structure," the use of age regression actually "permits the resolution" of the issue at hand.

TYPES OF MEMORY

When working with age-regressed patients we are always confronting the topic of memory. Revivified memory feels even stronger than commonplace conscious memory – both therapist and patient, reared in a society of documentation, are drawn to the perennial question: Is that exactly the way it was?

Yes and no. Memory has been poetically described as a "cloak constantly in process of renovation, sometimes with gross additions of new material" (Greenacre, 1975, p. 50). The electronic revolution has been kind to the researcher. No longer need theory remain abstract in the field of memory. The more that child development specialists observe the earliest stages of infancy, aided by sophisticated automatic video equipment, the more they are able to observe the effects of memory in action far sooner than was imagined. Recognition memory, for example, in which the subject interprets a current event in terms of a remembered past association, has been observed in infants of just ten weeks (Kagan, Kearsley, & Zelazo, 1980, p. 64)! Even just a few days after birth it has been determined that babies turn their heads towards pads soaked in their own mother's milk discriminating – namely, remembering – which smell belongs to the breast they already know (MacFarlane, 1975). Likewise, as Carpenter, Tecce, Stechler, and Friedman (1978) have demonstrated, babies are able to regulate "visual input differentially related to the experimental stimuli; in particular, by the age of one month they are able to discriminate their mother's facial features from those of strangers, meaning that they can, at least to some extent, remember their mother.

Evocative memory, namely recall which exists without the presence of a stimulus to prompt it, is thought to occur somewhat later, perhaps after the development of rudimentary language or some other means of symbolic encoding; Nachman and Stern (1984) provide a good review article on research into that subject. Anecdotal data continue to con-

found theory of early memory; the following examples have
interested those puzzling over this issue. At age 11, my
daughter Nancy described in accurate detail a red-haired doll
she received for Christmas at the age of 17 months. Its head
fell off within a few days, and an exchange for a blonde
replacement, dressed differently, was effected. Although
Nancy could not name the colors at 17 months, she could, at
age 11, name every color of the original doll's hair and dress
accurately, "seeing" it in her mind's eye, and applying her
current knowledge to the original scene. Curiously, at 17, she
no longer "remembered" the incident when asked; it was as if,
having been expressed, it could be dismissed from early retrieval. However, during that later conversation she then
spontaneously recalled having once slept in a large, almost
bare room, one used now as a playroom. For the convenience
of the baby nurse she had stayed there for the first few weeks
after coming home from the hospital, a fact we had never
mentioned to her. "All that air!" she exclaimed, when I asked
her what she remembered from that time.

So much for the inability to recall what has been experienced preverbally. It appears that human beings are able to
overlay cognition later achieved onto earlier events, which
are then retrievable in verbal form. To understand the construction of memory is obviously far more complex than to
observe and describe it. It will benefit us here, then, to dis-
tinguish and catalog elements of the term further.

Memory can be divided arbitrarily into the following categories:

(1) *Memory without significant affect*, which would include memory of commonplace events producing little or no affect in the subject (I remember what I ate
for an ordinary breakfast today);

(2) *Memory of past affect*, currently without significant
charge, such as memory of events that were once
emotionally important but now seem to be completed
(the first day of kindergarten; an argument with a
friend; a death fully mourned);

(3) *Memory with mostly isolated affect or with totally blocked affect*, sometimes accompanied by partial or full amnesia (as in a catastrophic trauma, or, more commonly, as in a death unmourned);

(4) *Distanced memory with "appropriate affect"* usually somewhat less than was first experienced (as in the expression of sadness, including, perhaps, some tearfulness, at the memory of a past death that the person seems to have fully mourned). As will be discussed later, there is usually some isolation of affect to be pursued in such instances. In addition, of course, there is

(5) *Lack of memory* — psychological amnesia, to be discussed separately (see the case of Stan, Chapter 6, for example), which is considered likely an extreme form of the blocked affect (type 3); and

(6) *Current memory* of events in the recent past still in active process.

The goal of age regression is completion, most commonly through revivification of memory followed by appropriate psychotherapeutic intervention. On the one hand, age regression can attempt the completion of a circumscribed, perhaps traumatic event, usually located in the distant past; as will be discussed in later chapters, this event can have occurred during the preverbal as well as the verbal stage of development. Or, via age regression, especially when linked with hypno-play therapy, one can attempt the completion — perhaps the total construction — of a developmental stage. We are, perhaps, most familiar with — and sometimes most wary of — the abreactive aspect of the first type of completion, in which a serious trauma is recalled and relived, sometimes with dramatically obvious seemingly positive results (though sometimes with damaging after-effects; see Chapter 11). We will discuss that category later (see Chapter 6). However, more commonly, the completion is much more limited in scope; often the memory may be easily recovered, or even part of conscious thought, a tale told easily, but without feeling (see memory type 3), as in the case example of Mi-riam; or, it may appear to have been well-handled (see memo-ry type 6), as in the case of Lara; or, it may seem trivial, as in the case of Mary. The pursuit of memory can nevertheless lead to significant and immediate results.

MIRIAM: GOODBYE, POOR BUNNY

Miriam, a bright, attractive 68-year-old woman, looking far younger than her age, became attached to the stuffed animals in the therapy room, purchasing one for herself. She found herself thinking about her lack of such toys as a child, but recalled that she received several live animals, such as rabbits and chicks, as Easter gifts. She remembered their presence, but not their loss, having no conscious idea about what had happened to them. In trance, she visualized herself first with a kitten, then with a rabbit. Note how Miriam maintains a dialogue between her active observing ego and the little girl self:

P: I can see myself. I don't like myself very much. I do mean things to the animals. I'm using a syringe to give a kitten an enema. Like was done to me. . . . And I see myself in the backyard. There was a small area under the back steps. . . . I have a memory of a white rabbit.

T: (Handing her a stuffed rabbit) And here's that rabbit. How do you feel?

P: Right now I feel tenderness, but I think what little Mi-riam felt was exasperation.

T: If it would be all right, you can find yourself going deeper, moving even closer to little Miriam. (P. yawns, for her an idiosyncratic sign of deepening trance.) You're stand-ing right next to her, and now, it is as if you are melting into her body. Big Miriam can watch from outside. How old are you?

P: Six or seven.

T: . . . six looking ahead to seven, seven remembering six –

P: I might be exasperated with the rabbit. . . . Part of me wants to bolt and run, to say I can't do it.

T: Part of you says I don't want to do it. Asking your unconscious now, if it would be okay to go on, you can go deeper. If it is not okay today to go any further, you can come awake.

P: (Yawns again, moves hands around stuffed rabbit.)

T: Your fingers know how they feel. Whatever they need to do, feel it through your fingertips.

P: (Moves her hands around rabbit) I feel like hitting it, but I don't know if I'm thinking that because I know it's just something children do. I hear my mother's voice and I'm hearing my own voice imitating her: "What do you *want* from me! You're killing me. I'll soon be dead, then you'll be happy." It's my way of working it out. It (rabbit) has to go in the doll carriage. (T. brings over doll carriage; P. puts rabbit in carriage.)

T: Do you need anything else?

P: A cover. (T. gets a towel. P. puts rabbit in the carriage and holds it down with the towel.) (In a loud voice) You *will* do what I tell you to do. You stop wiggling! You stay where I put you! I want you to do what I make you do!

(Miriam acknowledged that the rabbit probably died, though she felt that all of the animals she had had "were just taken away" behind her back. Burial had never been a possibility.)

T: What do you want to do now?

P: Bury the rabbit.

T: Would you like me to help you dig a hole? (P. nods, moves her arms in a digging motion.)

T: Now we put the dirt on top. (P. moves her hands.) Is that all we need to do?

P: Put a stone on top.

T: Good. What kind of stone is it?

P: A stone, just a stone I picked up.

T: Now you need to say goodbye.

P: (In a flat voice) Goodbye, poor bunny. I'm sorry I wasn't very nice to you. That's the problem. I don't feel anything, just empty. (P. puts her head on T's shoulder and sobs.) I feel very sad for that little girl. I didn't even let myself get attached. I feel so sad. (Cries, then suddenly blinks and opens her eyes) Shame suddenly turned into sadness!

Miriam found that claiming the sadness for herself relieved her of the shame of that memory. The theme of shame in her life then became the focus of the session and of subsequent sessions, during which cognitive understanding of the deficiencies in the parenting she had received replaced an unconscious shame in what she felt to be deficiencies in her being.

LARA: AVOIDANCE OF LOSS

Lara, of Armenian descent, came to therapy in the throes of indecision regarding a choice between two romantic relationships. Attractive, pleasant in manner, and vocationally productive in a professional field, she always found an intelligently reasoned argument for the other side of any decision on that subject. I wondered if the issue was that of inability to face loss. In a hypnotic state Lara fantasized scenes in which primary process predominated: fires, witches and dragons, giant machines, a tiger fish. She saw herself as composed of two parts, a "lighter part" and a "heavier part," the latter being "full of horrible dark syrup, like Godiva chocolates. I hate Godiva chocolates. Ycch! Tastes terrible." She chose to dispose of them in a cemetery.

The following scene emerged:

P: I'm in Greenwood cemetery, that's where my grandparents are. A beautiful cemetery, has a little pond. . . . Now I'm driving away in a hearse.
T: How do you feel?
P: I'm sad, but it's sadder to go to their house. A cemetery is just a place for bones. They're coming out and waving goodbye.

T: Can you say something to them?

P: They know anything I would say. (avoiding)

T: Sometimes it's good to feel the words in your mouth anyway.

P: The hearse is just driving on. (more avoidance)

T: Perhaps you could have it go around the block, so you could go back and say what you have to say.

P: (Pause, followed by a long stream of words in Armenian, probably several paragraphs long) You see, they knew that (a few tears, the first shed in therapy).

T: Is that a good feeling? (My own wish that it be a good feeling sneaked up on me. A neutral inquiry would have been more appropriate.)

P: It's sad, but it's good to feel that.

Thus it seemed confirmed that avoidance of loss was important in Lara's psychological structure, although the loss of her grandparents, per se, did not appear to be pathogenic. Investigation of other losses would therefore become a focus of the agenda of the continuing therapy.

MARY: BLOCKED AFFECT

Mary's husband had an acute medical crisis involving emergency eye surgery. The surgery was successful and no further difficulties were anticipated. After a few days in the hospital, the husband returned home to a brief convalescence, during which some minor assistance from the wife was required. He then returned to full activity. The patient seemed to have weathered the event well; she expressed her anxiety openly, cried when anticipating the surgery with its possible ramifications, including the ever-present, though unlikely, possibility of death, called on her friends and family for support, allowed herself to accept the minor feeling of irritation from the additional chores the situation put upon her. Nevertheless, she came in with what she considered a psychogenic sore throat that had persisted since her husband's return home.

Recounting the event once again, Mary was encouraged to speak louder, and then even louder. Shortly she was reexperiencing the fears and anticipatory grief she had felt before the surgery. She found herself crying with abandon, making the amount of noise she had felt inappropriate to a hospital setting, where she was trying to behave with some decorum, or with her children, to whom she was the emotional support, or, after the fact, with her friends, whom she felt would view the situation as one that had ended happily. Immediately after the session the sore throat disappeared. The completion of inhibited affect eliminated the symptom, seemingly by magic.

This experience being fairly easy to retrieve, the above vignette is an example of the fourth type of memory where, although not readily apparent, there is, in fact, some blockage of affect, at least of the intensity of affect. Formal hypnotic induction was not necessary and play therapy was irrelevant; the event was recent and there was little resistance to the resolution of the difficulty. Although rarely identified as such, this is, in fact, a simple example of the use of the (informal) induction of regression. Here, regression served preventive purposes, excising the symptom before it became fixed.

The reader may recall many similar situations with patients, in which the regressive process seemed to occur without the conscious planning function of either therapist or patient. Ferenczi (1980a), for example, describes the results of what he viewed as an extension of free association, as he "urged the patient to deeper relaxation and more complete surrender to the impressions, tendencies, and emotions which quite spontaneously arose in him." If one comes from the knowledge of age regression, the reactions of the patient are predictable: " . . . the freer the process of association actually became, the more naive [one might say, the more childish] did the patient become in his speech and his other modes of expressing himself" (p. 129). The reader may even hesitate to categorize such fairly common occurrences as same-generation cousins to hypnotherapy. Nevertheless, I contend that they are. For when the therapist moves with the process, true age regressions develop as, in fact, they do and are reported in the rest of Ferenzci's paper, in which Ferenzci cites sessions in which the patient and he enter into what he calls "a game," "perfectly analogous to the processes described to us by those who analyze children," in which early scenes of "traumatic occurrences" are "revived." Ferenczi, not having deliberately induced hypnosis, nevertheless labels the patient's state as that of trance.

We might hypothesize, for example, that through free association (what Bower, 1981, terms "associational chains" based on affect), through the existence of mood-dependent memory states, and perhaps through spontaneous affect bridges (a term coined by Watkins, 1971), previously dissociated memories could be revived. Thus, without the deliberate process of formal age regression, such age regression can and does occur; the elderly patient, consciously recalling and describing Christmas at age ten, rhapsodizes, "I remember Grandma's cookies – I can actually smell them now!" The deliberate use of hypnotic technique merely structures and makes efficient a process that is probably as old as humankind itself. Even little Nichette, with no training at all, knows that the Queen needs lessons in playing from someone who loves her. No therapist need feel like a stranger in a strange land. Even those practitioners who have been unfamiliar with the formal induction of trance will readily find parallels in their own work to the cases to which we will direct our attention in the following chapters.

5

HYPNO-PLAY THERAPY
FOR THE NEUROSES:
A DEVELOPMENTAL APPROACH

Hypno-play therapy can be extremely effective in working with patients for whom the root of their neurotic suffering is in a developmental failure, usually a failure of the environment. There is no neurotic condition for which such treatment might not, in certain cases, be relevant. In this chapter we will see its application to cases of isolated trauma, early developmental gap, pre-adolescent fixation, delayed grief, and stress. The reader will surely be able to supply countless additional categories in which a similar approach would hold.

Among the countless definitions of neurosis I prefer that of Andras Angyal (1982): "Neurosis is not a partial disturbance limited to just one province of personality. Neurosis is a sweeping condition . . . , a way of life" (p. 71). This broad view holds that a neurotic condition does not remain constrained to one sphere of a person's life, sealed in on all sides in a leak-proof poison gas canister. Rather, the anxiety associated with the neurosis seeps insidiously into all areas of the person's experience of the world. No matter how narrow and apparently circumscribed the complaint, we can be confident that the "narrowing in" process – from which the word anxiety derives – has affected the person to the extent of preventing uninhibited development. Even an isolated trauma—say, a snake bite in Viet Nam—may lead to a fear of snakes in New York City, a *phobic* fear of snakes in a climate in which snakes are unknown. Such a phobia might, hypothetically, touch off a panic reaction to the AMA insignia, to a movie about Africa, to entering a toy store (with rubber snakes). No matter how seemingly irrelevent or inconsequential the phobic object, what is important is the latent fear, with the unconscious hypervigilance engendered by it. The person with a simple phobia rarely comes for treatment, not recognizing its toxic influence; however, while working with someone around what seem to be other issues—a divorce, a feeling of a lack of success in a career—the more "limited" phobia may be mentioned peripherally by the patient (see the case of Tom below). Then one begins to see the wisdom of Angyal's formulation.

The point is that a neurosis affects all of a person's life and, by extension, the lives of those in that person's interactional system. Adopt any angle of observation—any theoretical stance—and there it is. It doesn't much matter from which position one starts—as in doing a jigsaw puzzle, sometimes one orientation may catch the eye, sometimes another. But the totality will emerge the same, from any direction. All roads will lead to Rome. A neurosis is a neurosis is a neurosis.

THE ISOLATED TRAUMA

In the following relatively simple example, a patient was troubled by a limited phobia which had a specific origin. Notice that the trauma did not have to be shockingly horrifying to be important in the life of the affected person. However, because the trauma was of ordinary proportions and was a one-time event, a little hypno-play therapy went a long way.

LORRAINE: PUBLIC SPEAKING PHOBIA

Lorraine, a brilliant scientist, asked for help with a phobic avoidance of public speaking. Because of this phobia she was unable to teach or to lecture on her many accomplishments;

her professional advancement was therefore limited. She had had a successful long-term course of psychoanalysis many years before; however, this issue remained untouched. She believed that its origins were in an incident occurring in the ninth grade.

Lorraine remembered the incident well, and showed mild agitation around it in the telling, done in the conscious state. Coming from a "progressive" elementary school, where she had been praised as an outstanding and creative student, she then entered the ninth grade of an ultra-conservative private high school. There, volunteering to read a report of which she was proud, she was humiliated in public for her unconventional performance.

While Lorraine went into a light trance state, I recounted the story she had told me a few moments before, using her own words as much as possible. By use of the screen technique (see Chapter 8) she entered the classroom where the event had occurred. Reexperiencing the shame and humiliation of the teacher's disdain, and of the class's rejection, she felt 13 years old again.

I asked Lorraine if she would like my support—an adult to keep her company in the classroom and to help her. After all, it seemed a bit unfair for her to have no champion in such a hostile environment. Together we constructed a suitable fate for the teacher: After playing with various possibilities (shooting her through the window like a missile seemed especially appealing), Lorraine decided to tie her to a chair and "disintegrate" her into a box to be shipped to Hawaii, where the warm climate might cure her of her cold-heartedness.

In that spirit, moving in imagination with Lorraine, I sent for the UPS man, and Lorraine labeled the box in a stroke of 13-year-old genius: DEAD RAT! We had a good laugh as, in mutual fantasy, the package was picked up. I volunteered to explain to the shocked delivery man that the contents of the package consisted of a scientific experiment. Within a week Lorraine accepted a speaking engagement which she executed successfully, armed with the suggestion of summoning up the vision of that box should panic threaten.

THE EARLY DEVELOPMENTAL GAP

Situations calling for a brief "corrective experience" are common in the practice of most psychotherapists. Age regression, with the component of play therapy as an option, often provides a satisfying brief and effective approach. Brown and Fromm (1986) offer a case in which an adult patient, during a hypnotic age regression, became a grammar-school girl struggling unsuccessfully with subtraction. The therapist, experienced in child therapy, was advised by the supervisor to treat the patient exactly as if she were a child unable to do her "take-aways." In behavior as literal as that of hypno-play therapy, "he presented her with an (hallucinated) arithmetic book and asked her to stand up and work out the problem on the blackboard. He patiently tutored her to the point of providing her with an emotionally corrective experience before terminating the trance" (pp. 70–71).

Commonly encountered psychotherapeutic situations involve the patient who presents with a difficulty or symptom which seems to relate in an obvious way to a particular developmental period, rather than to one traumatic childhood event. No matter what comes up for consideration in a session, it always seems to relate back to that one period. That stuck place, sometimes referred to as a fixation point, is often a time when, for some reason, the developmental needs of the patient were not met, or not met sufficiently. The synonymous term, a developmental "arrest," need not, as Sullivan (1954) notes, "imply that things have become static, and that from thenceforth the person will be just the same as he was at the time that development was arrested" (p. 217). Rather, it is later on that we see "the appearance of eccentricities of interpersonal relations" which betray "signs of developmental experience which has been missed or sadly distorted" (Sullivan, 1954, p. 218). The fixation point can also be seen from a multi-leveled perspective. The person looking back, reinterpreting his or her history, might even identify the embryonic beginnings of such an "arrest" before its definitive appearance.

Thus, the neurotic person goes on living, perhaps more successfully than not, either (1) somehow always getting into the same sort of trouble, feeling the same sort of dissatisfaction with a kind of fateful regularity, or (2) finding life constantly mediated or even stopped by certain patterns of avoidance. Viewed psychoanalytically, the former life orientations termed the repetition compulsion, and the latter, the avoidant or phobic adaptation, are opposite sides of the same coin: a means, obsessive in quality, of dealing with trauma (occurring, according to Freud [1939, p. 74] before the age of five).

The "positive" function of repetition compulsion is an attempt, as Freud argues, "to bring the trauma into operation once again—that is, to remember the forgotten experience or, better still, to make it real, to experience a repetition of it anew, or, even if it was only an early emotional relationship, to revive it in an analogous relationship with someone else" (1939, p. 75). Thus, from a functional view, the repetition serves the purpose of making the problematic situation available for solution. The car must make the noise before the auto mechanic can identify the difficulty!

The avoidant side of the solution, labeled "negative" by Freud, is populated by "fixations with a contrary purpose" (1939, p. 76). However, we can look at phobias in the same fashion, understanding that at their root is the same yearning to address the issue to be treated. From both the positive and negative direction, the patient is unconsciously propelled to create the situation, in order to give us the chance to make the acquaintance of its cause and to plan a strategy for its repair. So the appearance of both phobia and the repetition compulsion can be a positive attempt of the patient to cure what needs to be cured.

This common situation is one of those for which regression to the cause and repair at the site of the damage are most appropriate. Where the original site of the fixation is early, play therapy may be relevant. The example below illustrates a situation in which the presenting issues do not appear to fall in the serious range and are not obviously of early origin. However, the history alerts the therapist to the possibility of an antecedent of a childhood separation anxiety disorder and the likelihood of a developmental gap.

TOM: A FEAR OF BEING FULLY ADULT

Tom, an intelligent, well-spoken single man of 35, presented around his inability to commit himself to a career appropriate to his college education and innate ability. He continued to work at a low-level, poor paying job, at which he was bored and dissatisfied. He was also disturbed at what he considered a pattern of avoidance of commitment to a love relationship; somehow, at the moment of permanence, he would "turn off." He later mentioned, but did not stress, the presence of a "mild" phobia about driving that kept him in a state of "slight" anxiety whenever on the highway. This phobia began after a couple of anxiety attacks many years before.

Tom's demeanor in the office was friendly and relaxed; he had many interests and several close friends, some current and some dating back to childhood. His father had died when he was 18 months. He reported good relationships with his mother, older brother, and stepfather, whom he referred to as his "father"; he had joined the family when Tom was four.

Tom would never have considered entering therapy for cure of the driving phobia, since, in fact, it did not seem to actually prevent him from accomplishing any of the usual activities of life. However, had it been more incapacitating, and had he come around that issue, we could have begun with the phobia as a focus. Nevertheless, we would have reached the same place: Tom's fear of being fully adult. To be partially adult was acceptable, just as was driving on slower roads. To be fully adult was equated with having a real job (rather than a make-shift time-waster) and a real wife (rather than girlfriend), with the responsibilities and decisions such would entail. At least at first glance, all of Tom's difficulties seemed to point towards that final step most commonly achieved at the end of adolescence: the separation from family and the attainment of adult individuation.

Thus, through the medium of hypnotherapy, the patient was directed to the time surrounding the unexpected death of his father, at age 18 months, which preceded his conscious available memory. The theory on which I based this intervention was that of normal development. Given Tom's capacity to relate to me with ease, and his reports of being comfortable in new situations such as interviews, I assumed successful negotiation of the period of "stranger anxiety" (seven to nine months), which has been shown to link up with "a general capacity for fearfulness" (Emde, Gaensbauer, and Harmon, 1976, p. 125). Finding no likely defect in that era, I went on to consider the next developmental stage, the so-called "practicing period" (ages 10–18 months); at this time "omnipotence" is the hallmark of the child for whom locomotion and primitive verbal communication have been achieved (Mahler, 1972, p. 491). This period overlaps with the fourth stage of object constancy (generally from eight to thirteen months), in which the child can maintain the "mental image of a vanished object . . . for at least a brief time while he conducts a search" (Emde et al., 1976, pp. 101–102).

Next the child enters what Mahler calls the period of "rapprochement" (roughly 15–22 months), with its "rapprochement crisis" centered around 18–21 months. "The junior toddler gradually realizes that his love objects (his parents) are separate individuals with their own individual interests" (Mahler, 1972, p. 495). Simultaneously, since the child has developed the (object constancy) capacity to "evoke a representation of the absent object and pursue it" (Emde et al., p. 102), it seems to follow that awareness of loss increases in kind. Parallel to that awareness, as the child "must gradually and painfully give up the delusion of his own grandeur" (Emde et al., p. 102), the child is increasing the ability for reality-testing.

Thus, the child typically becomes more aware of the feeling of separateness while becoming ever more independent. Again, of course, the child concurrently becomes ever more acquainted with frustration and helplessness; as Johnson (1985, pp. 19–20) puts it, "The child is vulnerable . . . to separation anxiety and the frustration of his dependency needs as well as to further erosion of his autonomy and self-esteem."

With those theoretical thoughts as background, I constructed a hypothetical base for the treatment plan. I noted that it was during this third period of individuation that a major upheaval in Tom's family had occurred, making it unlikely that this task was completed. I conjectured that a marital commitment implies accepting the risk of losing the new love object. Tom's original loss of his parent had followed the stage of image evocation (and its stimulation of the feelings of loss), but had preceded the completion of the task of object constancy, typically achieved between 22-30 months. Therefore, the foundation for completion of grief work was likely lacking.

Given this theoretical formulation, the choice of approach would be age regression with the likely addition of play therapy around the issues of loss and separation-individuation. Theoretically, one would, for example, include stuffed animals to be loved, left, and loved again; blocks with which to build, destroy, and rebuild; cars and trucks to come and go; and games involving hide and seek. The expected result for such an adult would include improvement in the driving phobia and its symbolic twins, noncommitment in the personal and career areas.

However, the above treatment plan never came to fruition. The use of trance with Tom brought forth few images relating to loneliness during childhood. Expansion from these images from which play therapy might have developed did not occur. Instead, Tom's direction turned towards relatively sterile productions, with markedly less content than conscious work. In the last of his hypnotherapy sessions he reported no images, but felt extreme anxiety, leading to a wish to "bolt." I therefore hypothesized that early material was as yet too sensitive to be investigated, and proceeded with conventional, primarily supportive therapy. Tom termi-

nated after about six months, pleased with his decision to
enter a graduate program in a field we had discussed. To my
surprise, a few months later he let me know that he had
married. Somehow we had done enough for the time being,
although I wonder if the unaddressed driving phobia remains as a red flag to yet unfinished business. I expect that
Tom will reenter therapy with me or with someone else,
when he becomes aware of whatever constraints still may
bind him.

The case of Yvonne, presented next, offers a clearer illus-
tration of a developmental arrest. The age of that arrest,
however, makes the decision for the use of play therapy a
close call.

YVONNE: GETTING OUT OF HER CHAIR

Yvonne's physical appearance and dress evoked the image
of a strong, athletic straight-shooter who approached her
profession and her sports activities with focused determination. A 30-year-old architect, she was referred for therapy
with symptoms of moderate depression and anxiety concerning the terminal illness of a former woman teacher: In the
initial words of her first session, she said that thinking
about this situation made her feel uncharacteristically
"scared," and that she was aware of feeling "tears in my stomach." A few sessions later, she reported a dream in which she
felt a sense of "desperation" when she "had to get up and go
somewhere, but couldn't get out of the chair and do it." She
seemed to function well at her work, and maintained a few
stormy long-term relationships with other women. Although
living a great distance from her family, she maintained contact with both parents and her younger siblings, mostly
around holidays.

Yvonne never had a sexual relationship with a man. She
identified herself as a lesbian; she had maintained a homosexual relationship with that teacher (whom she referred to
as a "second mother") since elementary school. This relation-

ship had evolved from the teacher's caretaking during a sports accident in which the then 11-year-old child had injured her ankle. The emotional part of the relationship had continued to recent times.

Within a few weeks, the patient appeared at my office on crutches; she had injured the same ankle. It was clear that this acting-out was a reconstruction of the original scene, a test of me (would I seduce her?), and most of all an expression of the need to complete a partially experienced focal event. Using hypnosis, I age-regressed Yvonne to the age of 11, choosing to direct her towards that period because of her strong affect around that time; when she would discuss the deteriorating condition of her teacher, she would look anxious, and say "I feel like I'm about 10 or 11 when I talk about it . . . dizzy . . . I feel like I'm going to be sick . . . my heart is racing. . . ."

In trance the patient alternated between recalling and reexperiencing her home life at that time: She spoke of the atmosphere as one in which "children should be seen and not heard," in which she felt she was to "make myself scarce," to avoid "rocking the boat" around her mother's "moods." Without explanation, around the age of 10 or 11, Yvonne's mother began to stay upstairs a good deal of the day, to be absent for breakfast, to be irritable when the child came home from school, to press Yvonne about her academic shortcomings. Yvonne made no connection with the death of her mother's mother the previous year. In an out-of-sight-out-of-mind style of denial, grief was not openly claimed in her family: An infant's early death, the loss of grandparents, the death of Yvonne's childhood dog were to be "forgotten," not mourned; "You'll get over it" was supposed to suffice.

The tensions of the school week held through to weekends. Conflicts around lack of perfection in schoolwork led to attendance at "Saturday school" sessions offered by the private school she attended. It was at the description of those Saturday school ordeals (as she felt them to be) that Yvonne spontaneously entered trance, the suggestion having been given to do so whenever appropriate. She immediately became that little girl, feeling unloved and pushed out by her mother; although father lived with the family, he seemed to be absent from the picture.

As Yvonne reexperienced herself at 11, the need for someone to be kind to her filled the room. In the mutuality of trance state, it was natural to be sympathetic about her injury, commenting about how much it must have hurt, marveling at her facility with crutches. Out of trance, Yvonne continued to cry and began to talk about the teacher, how confusing her feelings had been when the teacher had applied first aid, touching her in the process. In the next few sessions, conducted in the conscious adult state, Yvonne began to claim the anger at the teacher who, she could see in retrospect, had taken advantage of a child's emotional neediness for the adult's own gratification. Yvonne's depression began to lift, and movement, such as application to a doctoral program, began to take place; she could get off the chair.

Throughout the rest of the two years of once-weekly psychotherapy, occasional sessions including age regression were interpolated with more frequent traditionally oriented hours. In one, for example, further grief at the lack of mothering during the latency and adolescent years was extended through my reading to her, while she was in trance, Eastman's picture book for children *Are You My Mother?*, thus linking, by implication, the younger needs of the preschool child to those of the older girl, for whom the use of play therapy per se would have been less appropriate. In another, Yvonne felt herself "falling backwards in time," once more regressing to that same 11-year-old era, feeling "dumb" and rejected, sitting in study hall: "I'm not doing so hot in school."

After revisiting (in reality) the scene of the camp in which the complex homosexual relationship had developed, Yvonne was able to grieve, weeping, "I feel like a huge chunk of my life is over." Then, in a hypnotic dream Yvonne felt the healing of old wounds, becoming a "kid again, walking through the trees, feeling the heat of the sun, walking around the cabins" of the summer camp at which so many bittersweet memories resided.

Unable to "block (feelings) out anymore," Yvonne felt the
pain she had squelched, then let go of it. Afterwards the
more adult-oriented therapy, with its current expressions of
old issues, could continue. Her sexual preference was no
longer being made by a victim, but by an open and mature
woman; it was a choice. Exceptional achievement in graduate school was realized; friendships with men and women
became less stormy, and relationships with siblings and parents less strained.

Eventually Yvonne was able to become conscious of the
imminence of "accident-prone" behavior and its correlation
with events paralleling the 11-year-old's feelings of abandonment. She felt that she was "becoming a woman," able to talk
to her mother without being overcome by "that little girl
feeling." The sudden death of her dog filled her with appropriate, expressed grief; after many months which she felt she
needed to complete that process, she got another dog. The
teacher died. Yvonne flew back for the funeral, joining with
friends who had known her for mutual support, revisiting
the scenes of their years together, both sadnesses and pleasures. Depression did not recur, just the "ups and downs" of
being alive.

In the four months set aside for termination, there were
no "accidents." Yvonne's grief was, in part, another revisita-
tion of the issues of abandonment with the realistic apprais-
al: "I feel like I'm losing a touchstone"; "I know that I will
miss you . . . I feel sad, but it doesn't feel like dependency."
"I'll miss your laugh." From the start a marathon swimmer,
Yvonne had begun playing other sports and finding a family
of friends from among her teammates. It would be hard not
to hear the metaphorical implications as, describing a game
of softball, she said, "I ran like I had no inhibitions. I got to
home. There was nothing but that moment!" At the last
session, Yvonne brought me a gift, a kaleidoscope; her card
described it as a "beautiful" object that "adds a richness to
seeing, and . . . has a rainbow of colors like the spectrum of
feelings of being alive."

At Christmas, six months after termination, Yvonne

wrote a note on a card in which Santa Claus is pouring forth piles of red hearts from his knapsack. She spoke briefly of the fluctuations of mood after termination, of her acceptance of her feelings thoroughout their whole range. She described her life as "a challenge, a joy, a struggle, all of that and much more."

This case is an example of the interface between age regression and hypno-play therapy. As an intellectually gifted 11-year-old, Yvonne was a bit old for play therapy of the usual sort; nevertheless, I served an adult role with the child for whom, for whatever reason, the parent was not available. Some of that work was done within the parameters of formal induction; at other times, the patient seemed to just slip naturally into that state without the boundary distinctions of induced trance.

The hypnotherapist will easily identify those moments when non-induced age regression has occurred: Just as even the untrained adult spontaneously uses vocabulary – and even voice pitch – with infants different from that which is appropriate with older children, the therapist's counter-reactions reliably identify the age of the patient. It would have been natural to have worked with Yvonne while playing ball or jumping rope with her, as many child therapists do with their preadolescent, sports-oriented patients; her injured ankle, however, precluded that, so talking as to an 11-year-old became the mode through which the healing of the original hurt could take place. Thus, the rest of the process, including the anger, the anxiety, and the loss connected with the mother's withdrawal, could be freed for perusal and completion. The preadolescent period, with its growing awareness of sexual identity, had been usurped. Therefore, treatment both in and out of trance focused on that general era.

Sexuality as an issue was not raised specifically until the second year of therapy, when explorations into heterosexual possibilities arose, along with other attractions to women friends. The evolution to this theme was a natural one. When the developmental barriers are lifted and normal development can progress, normal growth will ensue, without direct attack on the "problem." It was probably fortunate – though scarcely accidental – that Yvonne chose a female therapist. She had a loving, but nonsexual, relationship with me; it was a corrective emotional experience for her to feel safe in letting me give her a hug, or in giving me one without risking exploitation. In short, in becoming free to be herself at 11, Yvonne became free to be herself at 30. She was also then free to have her own struggle with her sexual preference from a base in which a child's hunger for a mother was no longer the dominating factor.

SEVERE DELAYED GRIEF

We often encounter patients for whom the presenting symptoms mask an incomplete grief reaction. Most often, of course, we look to the relatively recent past, several years back perhaps. Less often, but still familiar to most practitioners, is the case of adult grief delayed from childhood. In such situations, developmental injury is likely, and interruption of the normal developmental almost certain. Here again, hypno-play therapy can assist in the completion of both the grief work and the developmental process.

In the case of Otto, we see clearly the results of hypnotic revivification and hypno-play therapy in the reconnection and completion of the original disturbing affect.

OTTO: LIKE FATHER, LIKE SON

Seriously overweight, Otto, looking at least a decade older than his chronological age of 31, appeared for the initial interview barely able to move one foot before the other. Psychomotor retardation was also evident in his inability to speak in sentences of more than three words, with pauses of several minutes between each, and only in response to direct questions. I therefore decided to delay the usual questionnaire in favor of a verbal history, as he seemed too depressed to tolerate the impersonal exercise of filling out a history

form. Otto responded affirmatively to queries regarding every standard component of depression except sleep disturbance, which he denied. He reported being "not myself" for
over a month and said that his friends believed that his
depression had begun when his supervisor had yelled at him.
Previous to the depression he had been active in various
sports, and had regular contact with several close friends.
He communicated weekly with his mother, who lived in the
same town; in subsequent sessions he expressed approval of
her two-year-old marriage to a man he liked. He did not know
of any precipitating cause for the depression and denied any
recent deaths, traumas, serious illness, or emotional discord.

Sitting in the room with Otto I felt as if I were in the
presence of someone in deep mourning. Out of that feeling I
asked, "Did someone close to you die when you were a child?"
He registered surprise that I would "know" such a thing: His
father had been killed when he was seven, he said. (Later, I
was to discover that he had been eight at the time of the
death. As we will see, however, Otto "lost" his father the
previous year.) Of course, the anniversary of the death, coin-
cident with the Christmas holiday, was at hand. And, of
course, Otto had never grieved either as a child or as an
adult. Most telling, Otto said that he remembered almost
nothing from the age of eight to fourteen. Although, in fact,
with some prodding he was able to remember certain limited
events, his feeling was of a lost childhood.

This year was particularly apt for the occurrence of the
depression: It was the year of Otto's son's seventh birthday,
and concurrently, the first year in which his mother, now
remarried, could no longer be considered as his father's wife.
Additionally, Otto's promotion to a new job as an on-site
supervisor of construction of skyscrapers involved him in
issues of responsibility for life and death. Moreover, this
work, considered by his colleagues to be undesirable because
of its high stress component, strained both his intellectual
and his physical capacities. I suspect that this factor
strongly contributed to a situation in which his usual set of
defenses was rendered inoperable.

This is a scenario for which the use of hypnosis and age regression, with or without the direct application of play therapy techniques, is made to order. Here again was one of those all-roads-lead-to-Rome situations – though what the supervisor's anger had to do with it was not yet clear. Father had died of a heart attack at age 36, falling from the construction site at which he was employed and being killed by the impact. His father before him had died similarly, within a few days of the same time of the year. It is no surprise that Otto chose the same line of work, beginning at the laborer level. His father, also overweight, had habitually purchased sweets from the very same vendor from whom Otto now purchased his, in his upward weight surge. But there was one optimistic note: Otto was still five years from his father's age at death. In one sense, the repetition compulsion associated with the reliving of his father's life could be taken as Otto's attempt to understand the tragedy that had occurred and to identify with positive aspects of his father ("he was great!"); the depression could be reframed as a signal of his unspoken goal to live a different way, making time for his family and surviving his children's childhood as their father.

Something was incomplete about Otto's father's death; it was sufficiently powerful that partial amnesia for the events following it, for several years, had protected that core trauma. Over several months' time we returned through age regression to the period before the accident and to the last leave-taking. Daddy was in the driveway, on his way to work. Otto could see the car with all the details of color and model, the snow on the ground. "Don't go!" he begged. Perhaps in retrospect, he had some prenominition: "I'll never see him again."

Over and over we went back to this material. In discussing it in the conscious state Otto's affect was one of puzzlement, of partial amnesia. In trance, he would weep, mostly wordlessly, and I would speak to him like the seven- or eight-year-old child he was. I read (or told) him fairy tales with appropriate themes, using hand puppets to talk for him when he was mute. One finger puppet, for example, could own up to being "lonely," or "sad," or "mad," that daddy couldn't go to the school hockey game. Another puppet could commiserate, adding to the affect—"That sure would make me cry, if I didn't have a daddy to go to my games."

Soon Otto began reporting that between sessions holes in his memory had begun filling in—his favorite phrase was, "All of a sudden it dawned on me . . . " followed by such predicates as "that I was in the Boy Scouts for a while." He was elated: "It doesn't seem like such a big thing—but it's just coming back!" He began a medically supervised diet and exercise regime and started to lose weight.

In trance Otto continued to return to the problematic period, although the instructions were nonspecific, merely "to go back to a time that occurs to you." He recalled scenes from the first house in which he had lived; in particular, he felt the pleasure of playing with his father. But the family had moved to a bigger house when he was seven; probably due to increased financial responsibility, father had taken on a second job and was rarely home to play anymore. It was to his loss of his father's *presence* that the age seven, to which he had originally referred, was related.

In the conscious state Otto affirmed positively, "No matter what, I know I would never get two jobs!" Through the analogy of his own fatherhood he could see that a child might be angry with his parent for having taken a second job, becoming an absent father. His own anger was, however, hypothetical. He could theoretically agree that he might be angry that his father had allowed himself to get so overweight, knowing that he had a history of heart disease; again he conceded (theoretically) that he might be angry that his father had died prematurely, leaving him fatherless. Although the puppets continued to be "mad," nevertheless, he returned to the assertion that, "It's not right to be angry—how can you be mad at someone who's dead?" Even when he was unable to consciously accept any of that anger, this discussion was important as a preparation and an intellectual framework into which the discovery of his own feelings would be cradled.

Meanwhile, at work Otto became able to withstand criticism from his superiors, arguing effectively when he felt that his decisions were correct. He was able, for example, to refuse to work overtime when he had made other commitments with his family; prior to therapy, he would allow himself to be scheduled for such overtime and then miss the event he had hoped to attend, feeling depressed and doubtlessly reexperiencing the child's side of paternal absenteeism. Otto reported that he could now enjoy attending ballgames with his son; previously, he had felt sad at such events, thinking of how he had never had a father to take him to these father/son occasions.

Finally, the last piece emerged. On Father's Day, Otto's son made a card for him, which moved Otto greatly. In trance, Otto relived the first Father's Day following his father's death. All the children in the class in school were making Father's Day cards. Otto sat there, crayons untouched, thinking–feeling–his own lonely bereavement. Becoming eight years old again, he talked about the day, perhaps one or two days before the death, perhaps the very same day, when his father had given him a knife to hold while his father did some home repair. Otto had put the knife in his pocket. When his father discovered that Otto had put it in his pocket in such a way that injury was likely to result, he yelled at Otto and took the knife away. In trance, Otto cried out, "Why did you leave? Did you leave on purpose?" The little boy was sure that his father had left, and therefore died, out of anger about the knife, putting those occasions (perhaps even separated by days) together in the way children attribute causality. I gave Otto crayons and paper, suggesting that he could make his daddy a Father's Day card now. He wrote, "Dear Dad, I'm sorry." He was crying too hard to write anymore, but talked out the rest of the card, further expressions of his guilt about his irresponsibility with the knife.

In retrospect, we can see how the anger of Otto's superior, at just the intersection of the Christmas season and Otto's son's birthday, precipitated the plunge into depression. Perhaps, we might hypothesize, the boss may have used some of the very same words—"You stupid fool," or something like that. Otto became once more the little boy who felt guilty of his father's death and guilty about his anger at his father for dying.

As a child left to be the "man of the family" of many girls and an overworked, pregnant mother, Otto had no place to take his confusion and grief. The church preached love and forgiveness, teaching that anger is a sin. So Otto literally followed the best advice he could, "Just forget it." I do not think that I am exaggerating when I say that his policy might well have led to his death at age 36, and another generation of fatherless sons to repeat the tragedy.

REVISITING THE HEALTHY CORE

So far I have been addressing the use of age regression and hypno-play therapy to directly address a specific wound from the past. Just as the child therapist operates in this way with the distressed child patient, so the hypno-play therapist treats the adult patient whose damage dates from childhood. Another important use of hypno-play therapy is the revivification of specific times or developmental periods in which the person felt whole, nurtured, confident, alive in the world. If one accepts Freud's (1939, p. 74) precept that the neuroses most commonly have their roots in events between the ages of two and four, the opportunity for the return to and revivification of those early years, during which the foundation of relatedness and healthy functioning may have been well laid, can be significant. Starting from a health-oriented position, the therapist has the opportunity to work with the healthy subsystem: As Angyal (1982, p. 289) puts it, "The message [of nonpathogenic harmonious situations] . . . should be heard," and is best heard when the patient "is able not merely to report but actually to relive his childhood experiences with their original emotional coloring."

In the case of Bill, the fixation point to which the current issue refers is clear and at a preadolescent age level. However, in contrast to the case of Yvonne, active play therapy in trance state served an important role in the patient's development.

BILL: HYPERVIGILANCE RELATED TO RACIAL ISSUES

Bill, a Black man in his forties, came with two stress-related complaints: high blood pressure (180/90), for which medication had been prescribed, and hyperhydrosis. A highly visible administrator in an all-white bank, Bill often changed his three-piece suit three times a day, as it became soaked by perspiration, which also broke out on his face and palms. Needless to say, these symptoms were embarrassing.

We began with some simple training in hypnosis, with the goal of a state of deep relaxation. There was no plan to make use of age regression. Bill was an excellent hypnotic subject and enjoyed demonstrating his "exercise" at work. He also began to delight in the opportunity to talk about his life in his nonhypnotic sessions, having never done so before with either family or friends. The topic to which he returned repeatedly was the pain that he felt from his adult associations with white people.

Raised an only child in a near-totally-white rural community, Bill had felt comfortable and accepted; thus, he felt betrayed and bitter when, in later years, he was confronted by the slights and outright bigotry of white people. Traveling in the South he witnessed the unprovoked murder of a fellow student by a gas station attendant who did not want a Black using the toilet facilities. Soon after, he was erroneously arrested and eventually cleared of a serious crime—it had been the "they all look alike" syndrome. No wonder he sweated! Yet, here he was, seeing a white therapist, and by that very fact silently announcing his wish to put his racial experiences in perspective, to replace his self-protective armor against the white race with an appropriate, limited trust of particular white individuals.

One day Bill appeared directly after emergency surgery

on his hand, which had been mangled in a snow blower. He requested further work in hypnosis so as to achieve relief from the pain and to prepare for further surgery. The induction consisted of a suggestion that Bill leave his adult body in the office and go to a place where he felt comfortable, relaxed, and happy. Soon an ecstatic smile spread over his face—he was Billy, six years old, playing with his (white) friends and asking for a ride on the mail truck. As he put it later, it was a "wonderful reunion."

In subsequent nonhypnotic sessions Bill—whom I now called Billy—talked about these friends, laughing warmly abut his exploits with them. He requested further hypnotic sessions in which to explore even earlier periods, before the layers of acquired defenses had been necessary. He easily regressed to the age of three, to his everyday life, watching the lamplighters light the gas lamps through his bedroom window, awakening to the sounds of the coal and ice being delivered, playing on his ride-on tractor. Most important, he remembered playing with his (white) friend across the street, eating cookies at his house. Asked if he was "colored," Billy went to his mother with the question. His mother said that he was indeed colored; because of her casual attitude, he did not attach any significance to her response, returning to play happily with his friend.

In these remembered incidents we see both the root of Bill's health and his subsequent neurotic adjustment. Because of his mother's attempt to keep Billy at ease in his environment, she promoted his sense of trust of white people; yet, on the other side of the coin, she did not prepare him for the painful realities of the urban school to which he was later districted and of the wider world of adulthood. Both of his parents apparently functioned successfully in an all-white adult world. Accepting their views unquestioningly, as do all small children, Billy remained an innocent, a virtual lamb led to slaughter. As one successful Black professional wrote in a *New York Times* article, "Prejudice and discrimination . . . cause some to build their own cages and become their own oppressors" (Lewis, 1985, p. 70). The unprepared become the overprepared in a hurry.

The conflict between Bill's worlds of trust and mistrust led to the two distressing physical symptoms of which he was aware and, more importantly, to his acceptance of a life of careful self-restriction. He also felt inhibited and ambivalent in relation to his parents. How could he be angry at such protective parenting? Its source was clearly love and concern. To be angry at these good people felt too sinful to approach – actually potentially traumatic. The guilt Bill felt lurking was a reaction to the anger and aggression he feared recognizing. Slowly, Bill allowed these angry feelings to emerge, bit by bit, dose by dose. At each point, through age regression to that simpler time when the world was all right and he all right in it, he came more in contact with the safe place within him, a place he can take with him and integrate realistically into the adult world.

At the end of a year of once-weekly therapy, Bill had risen still further in his organization, his higher position entailing extremely high-stressed public appearances. Bill, the burnt adolescent and adult, did not forget the fire. He continued to play his feelings close to the vest. But his experience in therapy – the relaxation exercise, the work in age regression, and the regular continuation of psychotherapy culminating in group therapy – seems to have had the desired effect. To the amazement of his internist, Bill's blood pressure reads 130/70, without medication. He now maintains his high-profile job in one suit per day. And, to his surprise, he has on occasion found himself forgetting his vigilance at work – he described having done a little tap dance in the hall, cutting up with one of his white colleagues, forgetting to hold his formal demeanor together – "I just didn't care!" he said, looking quite amazed. He was not the only one, I'd wager.

6

HYPNO-PLAY THERAPY AND CHARACTEROLOGICAL WORK

More so than the neuroses, characterological (or personality) disorders are invisibly woven into human development. While in the neuroses a specific trauma or particular thematic issue has skewed the patient's life orientation, the character disorder *is* the patient's orientation. It is as if the patient has had a certain view of self and world actually implanted in his or her eyes. The person wearing glasses can remove them if they become bothersome, adjust them if they are ill-fitting, or replace them as age modifies the need; however, the characterological view is indistinguishable from the self and as such has the feel of permanency.

Additionally, since the formation of a character disorder is commonly believed to precede that of neurosis, the "character" or "personality" disorder is experienced as syntonic — it's how the patient has "always" been — it *is* the patient's person. What is more, preverbal experience is often crucial to the formation of the character disorder, and such experience is not as readily accessible to memory or to discussion as that of later periods. Lastly, the formation of characterological issues in the child may not be due to overt pathological behavior on the part of the significant adults in the family constellation. Much pathological behavior is covert — quiet, unobtrusive, private, as in the case of Barbara (see below). Other damage may not be due to any identifiable pathology of the adults at all, but may stem from empathic failure, that

76

is, the failure of the significant adults to respond with pleasure and acceptance to the baby's temperament. As Pine
(1986) states in his paper on the development of the borderline personality, "It is the child's experience of the stimulus
which must be emphasized; the stimulus itself may not be
externally identifiable as traumatic" (p. 452).

Were the theory of absolute critical periods literally correct, most of us would be out of business. In fact, I take the
somewhat extreme opposite view that most non-organic psychological damage can be ameliorated, and much of it almost
reversed, leaving behind, perhaps, some scarring, some
bruises, but little pain and few or no limitations on living. If
ignored, the sequelae to deprived and damaging childhoods
will not just go away like a bad cold. But, if they are attended to with care and educated attentiveness, major change
can be effected.

In this chapter I focus solely on the schizoid and chronically depressed adaptations to life; often, in fact, these orientations are inextricably bound up together. Other character/
personality disorders are represented elsewhere in the book.
To this date I have found none of these disorders, excluding
the antisocial, unresponsive to age regression and/or hypno-
play therapy. The same principles appear to hold regardless
of the disorder; as the roots of the pathology are in childhood, so are the means for cure.

THE SCHIZOID PATIENT

According to Guntrip (1969), the schizoid person is one
whose "original needy, object-seeking, and ego-developing infant psyche remains the basis of all psychic functioning . . ."
(p. 35). Often encountered in the psychotherapist's office,
such a person is, in some ways, the antithesis of the ideal
patient. Since relationships are "too dangerous to enter into"
(p. 35), this patient cannot join in a therapeutic partnership.
In the extreme the schizoid person is "an utterly isolated
being . . . unable to communicate with others and never
reached by others" (p. 220).

However, schizoid people are actually ideal patients for hypno-play therapy. First of all, they are likely excellent hypnotic subjects. Already inner-oriented, perhaps fantasy-prone, schizoid patients are expert in depersonalization, operating in life by making use of the phenomenon of mind/body splitting that is basic to trance state. The schizoid person is often aware of feeling deficient: As Larry (see Chapter 1, pp. 6–7) put it in retrospect, after having broken through in trance to the freedom of tears, it feels "awful to have something that's part of you, not to be able to break the barrier. It's good to stir up what's packed down way inside. Like in a lake, you stir up the debris down below." Through hypnosis one can often get below – to both the debris and the fecund soil – and eventually undermine the defense of depersonalization that estranges mind from body, making feelings alien to the overdetermined intellect.

Being literally out of touch with the corporeal self, schizoid patients lack a sense of membership in the human race. Such people cannot feel the expansiveness of creativity which, as Greenacre (1957) aptly notes, involves "sensory responsiveness to the individual's own body state" (p. 53). The schizoid patient is likely suffering from what Winnicott (1958f) called "unintegration" (as differentiated from disintegration), a state in which the infant "has had no one person to gather his bits together . . ." (pp. 150–151). To summarize with Winnicott's (1986a) words, "Be has to develop before Do" (p. 42).

It is important to remember that regression of a non-directed sort can lead to a feeling of panic, as schizoid patients may contact the utter emptiness of the core of their usually depressive being, a place to which they often refer as "the black hole." It is imperative to have play therapy as an option in working with such people. The simple addition of a stuffed animal or puppet (as in the case of Stan, below), animated by patient and/or therapist, for example, can form a mediating bridge to human connectedness that is close enough to comfort but not too close to bear.

STAN: "NOBODY LOVES ME"

At 50, Stan was referred for adjunctive hypnotherapy by his primary therapist. A thin, sallow man, Stan spoke in a small, toneless voice. He ducked his head when speaking, his demeanor was hopeless and withdrawn, and his affect was flat. He did not consider himself to be depressed, however; in fact, he did not seem to have any connection with his feelings at all. His complaint was of lack of memory for historical events in his life, and, more annoying to others, for ordinary data such as appointments, daily chores, telephone numbers, birthdays, and other such details about which life revolves. Complete neurological testing had proven negative.

Stan's work as a layout artist seemed minimally, if at all, affected by this memory problem. Although he was married, he spoke of his wife in the same tone of voice as used in referring to a piece of furniture. As he described their relationship, he and his wife seemed to co-exist, passing in the night, so to speak, rather than living together. He had no close friends.

Stan was an excellent hypnotic subject, going into moderate trance with the simple suggestion that his eyes could close when they felt ready to do so; arm levitation was suggested as a signal of deepening, and indeed, first one arm and then the other lifted at moments of increased affect. The following excerpt from the work in trance state typifies the sort of progress that marks significant achievement for the schizoid person: no large-scale dramatic discoveries, just the everyday, commonplace feelings that people normally integrate into their lives without great difficulty.

Preceding the trance, Stan had reported hearing "voices" in his head saying, "Nobody loves me." When questioned, it seemed that these were more akin to audible thoughts than to hallucinations.

T: Can you tell me where you are, Stan?
P: (Silence, approximately 30 seconds) I don't recognize it.

T: Mmhm. What is it like?

P: Just patterns. (Silence, again approximately 30 seconds)

T: How are the patterns now?

P: Changed. Now light and dark.

T: Good, let them change. (Long silence; second arm rises) Even your right hand is going into trance, your body knowing just how to do it.

P: (Breathing much faster, face becoming mobile)

T: It's all right to have those feelings, strong feelings.

P: I'm afraid.

T: What are you afraid of?

P: I'm afraid it will cause another upset with Amy (wife). I'm not seeing anything in particular. (In a higher, childlike voice) I don't like anyone to be angry. They yell at me.

T: Who's yelling at you?

P: My aunt.

T: Can you hear her yelling?

P: I can't make out any words. Doesn't matter, she looks upset.

T: She looks angry.

P: She gets all wrinkled in her forehead, her eyes get small, and she shakes her arm at me.

T: How old are you now?

P: Ten or twelve.

T: Can you let yourself get into that young boy's body? He has no facial hair yet, his skin feels different (arm rises further). How old are you?

P: Ten.

T: What month is it?

P: Summertime.

T: What are you wearing?

P: Shorts and a T-shirt.

T: What color are your shorts?

P: Grey.

T: If you look down at your feet, have you got shoes on? or bare feet?

P: Tennis shoes.

T: What time of day is it? Or night?

P: Afternoon, a little after lunch.

T: What did you have for lunch?

P: A bologna sandwich. Auntie made it.

T: Why is she mad at you?

P: (Louder) I don't KNOW!

T: Gee, I don't think I'd feel very good, not knowing why someone's mad at me.

P: (Nods several times) But she must be right.

T: She must be right?

P: That's the way it is, everybody knows the adults are always right.

T: What happens then? Do you say anything?

P: (Shakes head) Then she mumbles, and then she goes away, and I feel bad.

T: And the voices in your head say "nobody loves me." (Holding up the dinosaur puppet) It's hard not to have anyone to talk to when you're feeling bad. Rex has been lying right here just wishing he could help out. Maybe you could talk to him.

P: (To puppet) I don't know why people get mad at me. I didn't do anything—it doesn't matter if I do something or if I don't do something, I never do it right.

T: (Stroking P. with puppet, speaking through puppet) No wonder you get scared, you don't even know why anyone's mad. You just think they're not loving you.

P: I just feel bad. (Strokes puppet, cuddles it)

The reader will observe the emphasis on visual detail around the setting; from Stan's description of Auntie's demeanor, we see that he is visually oriented. Indeed, detail is particularly important for schizoid patients, who, having no sense of grounding from within, have anchored themselves in their attention to concrete, visual aspects of the environment, which they need to feel safe: Not knowing how *they* feel, they do not know how others feel without taking mechanical inventory of the observable data. For the same reason, I provide some of the identification of feelings, here translating "upset" into "angry," reporting how I would feel in that situation. The puppet – whom the patient had earlier appreciated for its nonthreatening lack of teeth – seemed an ideal choice as a combination of projective device and transitional object. The patient was able to tolerate and draw solace from touching and being touched by the puppet, where the direct touch of a human being would likely have been frightening.

It seems, perhaps, a small thing: A man remembers his aunt yelling at him. But that is not what this session was about. In this brief half an hour, Stan finally *felt* – unloved, frightened, and consoled. That is the work to be done with a schizoid patient – the introduction to his own feelings. As a postscript, the reader might like to know that Stan telephoned the next day to ask in what store he might find Rex's "brother." He chose to name it Rex as well. A connection had taken hold.

THE CHRONICALLY DEPRESSED PATIENT

What appears as lifelong depression, while not considered a character disorder per se, is one such life orientation. I am not talking about the endogenous depression of the affective disorder, the cyclical mood swing of the cyclothymic patient, or the exogenous "neurotic" depression in which the precipitant is more or less readily identifiable. Rather, I am talking of the state of mind of the person whose entire life is one of "quiet desperation," anhedonia perhaps occasionally punctuated by even blacker periods of complete despair with suicidal thoughts or behavior; an example of such a case (Marlene) appears in Chapter 3. The chronically depressed person is likely a social isolate, working at an uninteresting job at which a minimal salary is earned and for which there is no inspiration or possibility for pleasure or advancement. Suffering from anergia, lacking any energy in excess of that required to survive, this person is unlikely to have either any vocational goals or significant hobbies, even of the obsessive, nonsocial sort. Trudging along in life is as much as this person can manage.

We can conceptualize this situation by recalling the early developmental stages of the small child. After the genesis of trust in the first few months, the baby begins to become aware that there are "other" beings separate from itself: mother (or her substitute), above all. It is commonly accepted theory (see, for example, Ferenczi, 1980c) that the baby, in its original omnipotence, "thinks" that it has created that world; that is, other possibilities have not yet occurred to it. Winnicott (1986a) posits, in fact, that the very experience of adult creativity itself stems from the raw power of this early, albeit hallucinatory, image of success (p. 40). From this early symbiotic period the "social smile" response blooms, and reciprocal interaction with the closest caretakers evolves into its particular interpersonal pattern.

What Mahler (1972, p. 488) terms the "hatching out" process continues, with the lap-baby era progressing to the six-seven-month crawling stage. This heralds a period of differentiation as the baby extends its world further from the original source of supplies and security (Mahler, 1972, p. 489ff). Out of that dawning, appropriately, follows the "stranger anxiety" typical of the eight-month-old, and the beginning of baby's use of transitional objects to ease separation pangs from the original loved person.

Having already achieved the upright position of sitting, baby now typically becoming efficient at crawling; at first within close range of the protecting adults, baby now begins to move out into the world, exploring the goodies of the universe. Who can forget the ecstatic gleam in baby's eye as it discovers that most wonderful of all treasure chests, the wastebasket! And what could be more thrilling than the toilet bowl! As baby reaches the end of the first year, it pulls itself upright at last, and with frequent intermissions for parental refueling, baby's exploration into the seemingly endless cache of discovery is underway. This is the period termed "practicing," that stage which Greenacre (1957) so aptly termed the "love affair with the world," the indispensable antecedent of "great talent or genius" (p. 58).

It is from deficiencies and damage during this era that a

lifelong depressive orientation may evolve. Recall that I am not speaking here of the depression marked by sudden plunges from normality into black hopelessness, but rather that joylessness, that lack of sparkle that dulls the spirit in a pervasive, grey cloud of meaninglessness. The following case is presented here as a classic example of a life without the "love affair." I am obviously taking the view, as expressed by Rutter (1979), whose studies of early separation experiences led him to conclude that "the consequences of deprivation in the early years are far from permanent and irreversible," that "human beings are amazingly resilient . . ." (p. 148). Hypno-play therapy at the developmental gap was the main approach in this case; conventional psychotherapy continued the gains until their integration into the patient's adult life.

BARBARA: LEARNING TO WANT

At 42, Barbara would appear to most observers to be a friendly, suburban neighbor, well-spoken, intelligent, and kind. One might assume her to be a teacher or other helping professional, coming from a conventional background.

The oldest of five, child of a politician and a former model, she was 11 when another daughter was born; two brothers followed several years later. All of these siblings have attempted suicide during their adult lives, although none has succeeded. In the family history is the maternal grandmother's attempted suicide as well.

Herself unnurtured, Barbara's mother speaks of her yearning for a baby and looks back nostalgically on the symbiotic period of nursing. But babyhood was to be brief indeed. The first in a series of home movies portrays mother literally teaching six-month-old Barbara to walk; in this and later periods such movies find Barbara's expression one of resignation and depression. As physical child and putative adult, Barbara remained alone, autonomous, and rigidly independent, making solitary pies in the kindergarten sandbox while her classmates did whatever five-year-olds do with each other, entirely out of Barbara's world. As an adult, life remained much as it had been in that sandbox.

In addition to this inauspicious early childhood, as the other children were born Barbara became the assistant mother, thus continuing, through parentification, her separation from the world of the normal child. Further, home was not what it seemed: Within the elegant high-rise walls, parties verging on orgies occurred frequently, when Barbara was supposedly asleep. Barbara's discovery of explicit photographs of the guests involved in homosexual and heterosexual acts made her painfully aware of the involvement of her parents in this behavior. And most damaging, since the photographs had been hidden, Barbara was left holding a taboo secret. Barbara's father died when she was 20. When Barbara, as an adult, finally pressed her mother for a discussion of the photographs, mother dismissed the topic as unimportant and indicated that it was not to be pursued.

On the surface, Barbara looked good to those who met her. Since she was neatly and appropriately dressed, one would not guess that even shopping for clothes was done as a chore, her selections being chosen as quickly as possible, allowing no twinge of desire to surface. Obviously intelligent, she was well-read and well-spoken, although educated only through the high-school level and employed as a low-salaried clerical worker. From her ongoing depressive way of life, which she described as being "blind in one eye," she occasionally sank to even lower depths, becoming suicidal. Medication during such periods proved ineffective; over the span of 20 years, individual and family psychotherapy taught her to claim responsibility for her behavior but to be less self-judgmental. Nevertheless, she called her future an "empty possibility" in which she was "pedaling on a stationary bike"; she felt "hopeless," like "laying down and being dead." She saw herself as a "wrapped mummy," afraid of human relationships, an alien in a world where nobody seemed to understand her misery. If asked what she wanted, she would shrink back in silence. She did not know how to want anything for herself. She did not even have access to the feeling, much less the words for it.

During the first five months of Barbara's two years of therapy with me, I did not recognize the early roots of her depression. Probably distracted by the shocking quality of some of her mid-latency experiences, I concentrated on her reactions to the dawning of her sexuality, when, predictably, she became involved prematurely in sexual relationships with boys in junior high school. Divorced twice, she was ambivalent about men and sexuality in general. She now questioned her primary sexual orientation; neither lesbian nor heterosexual relationships had proved satisfying. We plowed along, likely doomed to the same lack of significant accomplishment as Barbara had experienced before.

Fortunately, Barbara's sister discovered a reel of home movie film and sent it to Barbara, who mentioned it to me. I was interested, of course; an opportunity to observe a client's childhood was not to be ignored. She brought it: There she was, from age four months to about three years. The scene was a setting worthy of *Better Homes and Gardens*; dressed in starched, ruffled dresses with Mary Jane shoes, Barbara, about six months old, is being pulled to her feet by her mother, propelled along the carpet, each leg manipulated into a semblance of walking. A few moments later we see Barbara, exhausted, lying on her back, holding and drinking a bottle. In later scenes, as she gets a little older, the camera follows her toddling through the house, grim, careful, alone. I remember feeling intensely depressed while watching this movie; Barbara, on the other hand, showed no emotional reaction to the film at all. It was just the way it was.

Thus, Barbara had not even had the opportunity to want to walk. Instead of the normal experience of infancy, in which the child discovers crawling, then, with a gleam in the eye, begins to pull itself up, to take a step holding on, to dare to let go, to fall and be encouraged to get up again, and, to the cheers of the adult, to take that first unsupported step, Barbara had never learned to want, much less to experience that basic, spontaneous pleasure at discovery and independence. As specialists in separation and individuation note, even without the parental pressure, "premature locomotor development, enabling a child to separate physically from the mother, may lead to premature awareness of separateness before internal regulatory mechanisms . . . , a component of individuation, provide the means to cope with this awareness" (Mahler, Pine, and Bergman, 1975, p. 4). It was Barbara's mother who had separated from her, not she from her mother. After lap-baby infancy there was no base of loving holding to which to return; the sense of her own magical omnipotence had been co-opted.

Given the information from the movie, at this point, five months into therapy, I decided to extend the therapeutic process into the region of play. The first hypno-play sessions were nondirectively oriented towards unspecified ages. In the following excerpt, one of Barbara's first excursions to childhood, she found herself experiencing the ages of five, and then one-year-old. Using the (movie or television) screen method (see Chapter 8) as a means to visualization enabled Barbara to see herself primarily as a social isolate.

T: Do you go to school?
B: Yeah (nods).
T: Do you like school?
B: (tips head) I don't know.
T: Do you play games? Do you like to have fun with your friends? You look like such a nice little girl.
B: I can see the playground at school, swings and stuff. It's like I'm looking at it.
T: Do you play on the swings?
B: No. I don't think so. Oh. I just watch.
T: Do you play in the sandbox?
B: Hm. Mm. (Smiles slightly)
T: Do you play with the other kids in the sandbox?
B: I don't think I play with anybody. I play in the sandbox at the same time with the other people. I like the teacher.
T: You like the teacher. What is her name?
B: Miss L.

T: How does she look?

B: She's pretty. Blond hair. Not really blond, light brown. . . .

T: Does she like to play?

B: I don't know. I just want her to pay attention to me.

T: Does she pay attention to you? Does she like you?

B: Mm. She thought I was a good girl . . . (Note shift of tense).

T: How are you feeling now?

B: Sad. (A few tears)

T: Do you know why you're sad?

B: No, just feeling sad. I don't feel like I belong there.

T: Feel lonely? (She nods.) Want some friends? (She nods.) Want the teacher to pay attention to you? (Nods) Will you go home and tell your Mom? (She shakes head.) Sometimes mommies can help you make friends with the kids. Sometimes they can hold your hand when you get scared, give you a hug when you get lonely. Think your Mommy could do that?

B: I don't think she wants to hear if I'm unhappy. Just good things.

T: Can you tell your Daddy?

B: I don't see much of him.

Continuing in the age regression, Barbara returned to seeing herself on the screen at a younger age, which she identified as one-year-old:

B: Seeing a little girl in the livingroom.

T: How little is the little girl?

B: One.

T: Where is the little one-year-old?

B: In the big fat chair.

T: Do you see the color?

B: Navy blue.

T: Is it soft?

B: Stiff and scratchy.

T: Stiff and scratchy. A lot of things in your life are stiff and scratchy. (Referring to an earlier comment)

B: I'm alone again.

T: Uh-huh, nobody else in the room?

B: Taking pictures.

T: Are you dressed up too?

B: No. In a nightie.

T: (Noticing how rigidly she is holding herself) Are you sitting very still for the picture?

B: Yes! . . . Comb my hair.

T: Does it feel good to have your hair combed? (She shakes her head negatively.) Does it hurt to have your hair combed?

B: It hurts! (Tears)

T: Makes tears in your eyes.

As Barbara appeared to be feeling more and more of the scene, I asked if she wanted to move into the screen. With her affirmative reply, using the induction model to be detailed in Chapter 8 (steps 5–7), I continued the process of her entrance into the screen:

T: You can let yourself move closer to little Barbara on the chair, and feel yourself getting into her body, just like melting, your arms, and your legs, and your torso. And as you feel yourself getting into her body you may stop understanding some things I say to you. Some words may not mean anything to you, just the grownup talking, you don't have to listen. Maybe "good girl," such a good girl, or "sit still and take your picture" . . . "comb your hair, just right, have to get the tangles out" (Barbara moans). "Now don't cry, smile, be a good girl, we're taking the picture." (She sits up straight, unsmiling.)

B: Go 'way. Leave me alone.

T: Do you want to have a nap? (She nods.) OK, all finished, go have a nap. . . .

Barbara had reexperienced a difficult and unpleasant time, and it was then important to do the healing work that play therapy can provide. It is helpful to do that work at the stage just preceding the developmental fault, shoring up the earlier stages of development, working into that time from underneath in a natural progression:

T: Getting smaller and younger. And if you can't talk you can cry, or kick, or laugh. . . . You probably won't know how old you are. (Long pause) Let yourself contract into that baby girl, like the shape of a letter V, smaller and smaller, all the organs of your body, everything is so much smaller. And your skin is different, and the air feels different on it. And your mouth feels different. A lot of interesting things in the world you can find out with your mouth. (In a playful voice) I bet you know your name, Barbara. When I say, "Hi, Barbara," I bet you know I'm talking to you! Hi, Barbara! (She smiles, then curls up, her appearance becoming more somnambulistic.) . . . You know, I like you! We can do all kinds of fun things. Can you stick out your tongue? Do you know where your tongue is? (She laughs.) I'm sticking out my tongue, can you stick out your tongue? (She does so and laughs. I laugh.) You play very nicely! I like playing with you. I like to play all kinds of funny games. You don't have to know anything about what I'm saying, you know I like you, don't you! (She nods and smiles broadly.) Let's play this game! (I more over to sit next to her and play taking off her nose with a lot of anticipatory fanfare. She participates by wrinkling her nose as I come near, and giggling as I catch it between my fingers.) Let's see, what's a good song to sing. (I sing, "In the Month of May," a song about a child's fantasy of orally-oriented fun — lemonade springs, a big rock candy mountain. She listens intently and then begins playing with my fingers; I play "this little piggy" with her. She hears my bracelet jingle. I take it off and throw it on the floor, where it makes a sharp ping. Each of us throws things on the floor, experimenting with different sounds.) We can have a real party throwing — who can make the most noise!

Barbara later described the experience of age regression as being "like falling," but she did not find the sensation frightening. My interventions were always small and gentle; using animal mitten puppets, I had little playful conversations with her, sometimes singing silly nursery rhymes, initiating preverbal games (as above) and making use of other such activities that encouraged nonthreatening contact. Remembering the findings of Stern (1985, p. 163) that children as young as 15–18 months have been observed to use signs and symbols, over the next few weeks I seeded animal stories with metaphors supporting the theme of learning to enjoy life; I particularly stressed the senses as vehicles, especially those in which gratification could be immediately and obviously enjoyed on a young level. In one story, for example, a group of animals had a party because they had chanced upon a weed that they found particularly tasty! As my office looks out on a wooded area and rabbits and other wildlife often pay unannounced visits to the picture window, the correspondence with reality was especially effective as a carryover into post-trance consciousness.

During the period of a few weeks after the initiation of hypno-play therapy, Barbara became increasingly proficient at maintenance of deep trance. Thus, we were able to expand into other activities in trance state, such as taking walks, picking flowers, window-shopping, and skipping down the street, activities which necessitated her being able to keep her eyes open while remaining in the hypnotic state, the visible evidence of which was maintenance of a catalepsy of one arm. At first Barbara was able to maintain this somnambulistic trance for about five minutes; later, however, it lasted from 15 minutes to a half-hour.

Despite this depth of trance, my attempts to use posthypnotic suggestion, no matter how embedded, had no directly discernible effect. Barbara always remembered the entire hour and left with a beatific smile; later she reported no particular change in her life or voiced doubts that she had been hypnotized, since she could remember the entire occasion. She said that at first she was participating because

"You're the boss and I should please you," but that actually, to her surprise, she had "had fun."

Barbara was puzzled and gratified when, a few days after one of the early "walk" sessions, a long-time acquaintance commented on how "warm" she seemed to be becoming. Shortly thereafter it "dawned" on her that "I don't know how to be close to anyone; I fight in every subtle way to stay uncommitted." Working with a dream in trance, Barbara saw the word FEAR printed across a screen; she associated the stomach pains she sometimes had with the fear of being known and not loved.

Depressive feelings continued to emerge regularly. Although Barbara never became actively suicidal while in therapy with me, suicidal thoughts continued to emerge: "There's such a hole in me . . . no hope. . . . I want to die. . . . Relief doesn't come anymore." Yet, in a few weeks she was talking about being "able to take a risk." Back and forth she vacillated: In one session she would recount a dream in which she felt "strong and capable," and in the next talk about "hanging on by the skin of my teeth" in order to resist falling into incapacitating depression.

A month later the seesaw shifted again. In a landmark session, in which she felt I had not been responsive to her felt need, she actually shouted, "You're not helping me!" She was able to recognize that she had a "want" (to be taken care of), and that this "want" was important to her. Having seen the film "Terms of Endearment," she recognized that she had always craved "the real intense contact" represented by being able to "fight" with someone.

In just another month, having serendipitously tuned into a television program about glass-blowing, she came into a session with a word I had never heard from her: "I got *excited* thinking about the 'what ifs' of doing that kind of work," she bubbled, saying that she had been "playing" with the idea of learning that craft. She actually drove about two hours to meet the artist and talk with her about the possibilities in that field — she wanted something and reached out to investigate. At the same time, to her good fortune, she was

let go by her employer in a reorganization of the office. Able
to survive financially by unemployment benefits, she walked
into a local stained glass studio and convinced the owner to
take her on for a month without pay, so she could try out the
skill. The work was not as pleasing as she'd hoped — lots of
cut fingers and not much creativity. Barbara gave it up at
the end of the month, but she did not get depressed at the
unsatisfactory outcome. Rather, she had discovered the joy
of feeling excited, and knew, now instinctively and from her
earliest levels of development, that there would be other experiences in which the fit would be better.

Sessions of conventional "talk therapy," including discussion of the here-and-now situations in Barbara's life, were
interpolated on an irregular, as-needed basis with hypno-
play therapy. More and more Barbara was moving in the
direction of creating possibility in her life. She toyed with
many vocational opportunities that she could pursue, given
her limited capital. The empty weeks of searching for work
orientation were difficult. In a note to me she wrote, "I can
still sense that there is a better way, that it is my own belief
system that has me trapped . . . but I can't grasp what I
need to do." Of life as an unemployed woman, she wrote, "I've
lost my sense of time. One day is like the next. Sort of a long
weekend . . . several weeks long. NOTHING appeals to
me . . . no work, no play, nothing that requires any input
from me. I feel exhausted, lazy, angry at myself, scared (so
very scared that this feeling will never go away), bored, dis-
connected, lonely."

From that discouragement, however, emerged a new idea,
rather than depressive defeat: launching her own business.
But even as she moved into action, researching the potential
market and learning how to set up a commercial enterprise,
she was given to bouts of the old depression, which continued to emerge around the many setbacks in the process, as
well as in relationships with her family and with her roommate. These issues, which felt more "adult" in quality, were
confronted in conventional talk therapy. The reader can assume that whatever style of psychotherapy is "normal" for

the therapist continues during such sessions, which help the
patient retain a day-to-day orientation in life. Additionally,
and importantly, the process of working-through, always essential to the solidity and lasting quality of psychotherapy,
must be done at *all* levels, from infancy through the present
age.

However, because of Barbara's recurrent depression, I
considered it essential to continue to build the base of
healthy experience through hypno-play therapy at the regressive ages, rather than simply to concentrate on the life-
changes being attempted. Thus, over the next few months,
in a process paralleling Barbara's developmental maturation,
I became even more of what Winnicott (1965, p. 75) called
"the environment-mother," who "wards off the unpredictable
and who actively provides care in handling and in general
management." Outdoor walks, in which Barbara remained in
trance, became at least a part of every meeting during that
time period, for this was a child for whom, as Winnicott
(1958g) noted, the family had provided the externals of child
care but had furnished insufficient nourishment of the baby
spirit. The adult's true self, so long hidden by the obedient,
half-dead false self, had suffered "an impoverishment that
derives from lack of experience" (p. 297). Intending to provide that experience by normalizing the act of sharing nature's simple pleasures, I hoped that the observations of
beauty, of curiosity, of the uninhibited movement of trees
and birds and small animals, would underscore the messages
of my "fairy tales." Since Barbara lived in an area not far
from the office, the very atmosphere could come home with
her, the more she was able to let it in through her pores.

Of all the senses, sound emerged as most central to these
sessions, as Barbara became newly alert to the varying
tones of the wind, the songs of the birds, the wind-chimes
hanging from a tree near the office entrance. Using a xylophone, I invented little songs to illustrate and accompany
my stories—a sort of impromptu Peter and the Wolf, in
which each character is assigned a unique musical theme.
Seven months after the onset of hypno-play therapy, the

child Barbara was no longer depressed and docile; regressed to age one-and-a-half she would strike the xylophone keys with me, would enjoy the clack of dominoes banging together, and could participate by making vocal imitative noises as we played with little trucks.

Soon Barbara's affect was sufficiently loosened that the three-year-old could play a game with blocks and various accessories in which each of us built and knocked down (with accompanying yells) our own and each other's creations. We had mock fights with the little dolls and matchbox trucks and concluded the session by pitching each item into the toybox with uncompulsive abandon. Barbara was becoming comfortable with wanting and even taking. It was lovely to watch her spontaneously reach for one of the xylophone mallets, experimenting with the tones individually ("Some sounds are like a flat tire!"), running the stick up and down the keys, and laughing at the possibility of making "angry" noises or "happy" noises.

Nevertheless, depression continued to reappear, although for briefer and briefer periods, and without the death orientation: I read some sort of hope in the metaphor Barbara used in now referring to herself as "an unbaked cake with a big hole in the middle – not good to eat *yet*" (emphasis mine). Concurrently, other growth was evolving. After difficult and painful emotional confrontations with her roommate, Barbara decided that her sexual preference was for men, although she liked "spending time with women." This realization led Barbara to feel "better and better," like having "shoes that fit right." The next session found Barbara sparkling with a surprise – would I like to see it? Out in the driveway was a moped – not only a way to save money on gas, but also a way to have fun doing so! Fun had become a legitimate part of life. She expressed feeling safe to "say what I mean." The best learning of therapy, she said, was that "you feel the way you feel" and do not have to "feel guilty about that."

As Barbara's business went through a seasonal hiatus, predictably there were more depressive moments, times that "the glimpses of myself being well [were] not clear anymore."

It was difficult for her to keep pressing forward to meet new people, to develop personal and professional friendships, and also to promote a fledgling business alone. Understandably, Barbara discovered that she did not know how to pursue a desire past its initial phase; having never had "wants" in the first place, how would she have learned to convert wants into realities! So we returned to age regression and hypno-play therapy, this time to what Barbara identified as age seven. Eschewing the manufacturer's diagrams, we experimented with building original and complicated structures with an erector set, setting out to make things that would "work," with gears, wheels, and pulleys. It was not surprising to find that simultaneously Barbara began to seek out and achieve publicity through newspaper interviews, leading to an immediate and almost overwhelming increase in the volume of her business! "There isn't enough time to play the things I want to play!" she laughed. "I'm in love with a whole lot of people and I want it all!"

Meanwhile, Barbara's relationship with her mother became calmer, as Barbara's personal boundaries became more distinct. What her mother did or did not say did not devastate her anymore; she did not have to own her mother's depression. She even "forgot" to feel guilty about not doing so. In addition, feelings common to most people began to have meaning for her. Although Barbara had shown little reaction to my two-week vacation the preceding summer, a week's trip that I took at this time led to her spontaneous realization of what she was feeling. "Oh, that's *missing!*" she exclaimed; having never dared to feel close, she had never been able to recognize loss. She was also able to weep with the grief of accepting that her mother "is not in touch with her feelings at all," and that this lack is at the base of her apparent disinterest in Barbara's life.

In follow-up, Barbara continues on a productive path. Her business is extremely successful. She has felt depressed at times, but has, upon identification of the specific trigger—usually suppressed anger, been able to resolve her feelings directly. She leads a normal life with depressive incidents, rather than a depressive life. Can any of us expect more?

7

A CASE OF AGORAPHOBIA
AND ACROPHOBIA

"I believe in hell. *This* is hell."

— An agoraphobic man

A REVIEW OF CONVENTIONAL THEORY AND
CURRENT TREATMENT METHODS

Most readers will be familiar with the classical psychoan-
alytically-based formulations regarding phobias. In general,
a phobia is considered as "a *symbolic* representation of the
potential danger" (Salzman, 1980, p. 106, italics mine) which
has been displaced and externalized from the original object
of conflict. Arieti (1979, p. 85) further refines this definition,
pointing out that "the phobia is not just a displacement . . . ,
but also a concretization of a vague or intangible threat," in
which a "global anxiety" is reduced "to a definite concrete
fear." Somehow, this concrete fear, becoming an *it* rather
than a threatening interpersonal relationship, feels more
manageable.

In particular, agoraphobia has historically been addressed
as a primarily female disorder connected with hysteria. As
far back as 1897, Freud, in notes and a letter to Fliess on the
topic of "The Architecture of Hysteria," spoke of the correlation of agoraphobia with a woman's "romance of prostitu-
tion," which, in some way not further elaborated by him at
that time, is considered to be the agoraphobic's "asserting

her mother's unfaithfulness" (p. 253). This focus on the female is, in fact, supported by demographics, which indicate
that between 66–95% of overt agoraphobics are women.
Chambless (1982) additionally observed that there is a bimo-
dal distribution of ages at which the illness peaks, namely
between 15 and 20 and between 30 and 40.

Although observable symptoms are clearly correlated
with obsessional thought patterns, agoraphobia has often
been associated with the diagnosis of hysterical rather than
obsessive-compulsive personality; as such it is frequently
viewed as representing the patient's unacceptable unconscious hostility toward the same-sex parent, and concomitant wishes for an incestuous relationship with the parent of
the opposite sex. Indeed, the man from whom the initial
quotation is taken harbored incestuous yearnings for his
mother and barely disguised rageful feeling about his father.

In *Inhibitions, Symptoms, and Anxiety*, Freud (1926, p.
127) tells us, here using the male pronoun for generalization,
that "the sufferer from agoraphobia imposes a restriction
upon his ego in order to escape an instinctual danger. The
instinctual danger in question is the temptation to yield to
his erotic desires. . . ." Being present "in the marketplace"
makes sexual temptations too close for psychic comfort; the
fantasy/wish/fear of seduction typically keeps Freud's (1906,
p. 350f) agoraphobic patient from freedom to walk in the
streets. In this interpretation, expanded in Freud's chapter
on "The Psychology of the Dream Processes," the agoraphobic patient's repressed libido bursts out into symptoms of
extreme anxiety and panic, which substitute for the original
conflict; "the phobia is erected like a frontier fortification
against the anxiety" (p. 581). The patient then experiences
an overwhelming sense of lack of control, with symptoms of
shakiness, faintness, heart palpitations, sweating, and physical weakness, which is translated as impending death or
insanity. Like its sibling mechanism, obsessional behavior,
which lacks the component of overt panic, the phobogenic
object (Freud's "concealed determinant") is isolated from its
meaning; in a case example from Freud's *Introductory Lec-*

tures (1916-17, p. 277), he comments that "However often the patient repeated her obsessional action, she knew nothing of its being derived from the experience she had had."

Even more so for the phobias—the phobic patient almost never makes symbolic connections during such an initial attack, for the multiple manifestations of terror are so overwhelming that the intellect is rendered useless. Behaviorists note that even a single panic attack is felt as a traumatic conditioning stimulus leading to "one-trial learning." In other words, the physical experience of that unbearable terror produces fertile ground for the almost certain creation of what they term the "conditioned avoidance reaction," which leads to a circular and ever-expanding morbid obsessional phobic system, sometimes including hypochondria and paranoia. The patient develops almost superstitious anticipation and practices what Salzman (1980, p. 60) terms "ritualized avoidance" of situations in which one might be helpless or unable to escape, thus creating "an illusion of power and control [which] may temporarily dissipate the anxiety" (p. 81). The fear, as identified by *DSM-III*, is that of experiencing the dreaded panic attack. Thus, what is generally called the fear of fear—the hallmark of the agoraphobic—comes to dominate the patient's way of life.

As a Freudian interpretation of the phobia would involve a highly taboo subject—incestuous sexual yearnings—it will be resisted for a very long time, during which, of course, the patient's life will become more and more constricted, and the family system more solidly organized in covert support of it. This syndrome is not surprising, since almost alone in what Chambless (1982, p. 15) terms "a morass of conflicting results" in statistical studies of the causes of agoraphobia and descriptive data about agoraphobics is the commonality of a history encouraging dependency and a life continuing that position. The likely choice of a mate is often based on what Hafner (1982, p. 82) calls "immature romantic fantasies" representing "an attempt to escape from an unsatisfactory family of origin." Compounding the situation, the secondary gains to the patient win a foothold: As Nadine (case follows) observed, phobias eliminated the awareness of loneliness by necessitating having people around her.

Due to both the patient's psychological avoidance of the issue and her understandable preoccupation with the physiological components of fear, psychological interpretations are rarely useful in the opening phases of treatment; as with pain patients, everything understandably revolves around the symptom and ridding oneself of it. Claire Weekes' (1982) popular manuals for phobics approach the issue squarely in that manner, referring to "the habit of fear," terming it "the important thing" to be addressed. She attracts the reader, doubtless the patient, by her direct, problem-oriented, forceful assertion: *"This must be cured"* (p. 7, italics hers). She chooses to totally eschew the psychological approach, supporting the behavioral theory that the "fear of fear, when it flashes almost electrically – as it does in a sensitized person – [can] be a cause in itself" (p. 16). She correctly accepts that an external orientation does not provide soil for an internally-oriented psychotherapeutic approach, and she therefore does not hesitate to accompany the patient in absentia (via audiotape, available separately).*

In extreme cases of agoraphobia, the patient is unable or barely able to come for her sessions. Nevertheless, the patient is desperate and, by implication, highly motivated, at least at first. Thus, the speedy interruption of the process from any angle is generally welcomed by her; the therapist, recognizing the damage that grows more and more convoluted with time, begins work from a symptom-oriented direction, occasionally even starting treatment for the totally mobility-impaired with home visits.

Given the patient's strongly conditioned fear of what have become mislabeled and overdetermined signs of physical arousal, the behavioral approaches have played a major role in treatment. These include relaxation training, hypnosis with posthypnotic suggestion, graded systematic desensiti-

---

*An excellent article by Andrew Musetto (1985) details an eclectic approach to treatment of the agoraphobic.

zation, reciprocal inhibition, paradoxical intention, shaping (with the mobilizing of positive social reinforcement), and *in vivo* practice or exposure (sometimes, though rarely, including the controversial "flooding" technique) with therapist or assistant. These procedures are often supplemented by lay or professionally-led support groups with formerly phobic members.

In addition, antipanic medications, such as the benzodiazepine alprazolam (Xanex) and beta-blockers, which prevent the physiological symptoms of panic, have been found useful in some cases, especially for encouragement of the initial foray into phobic territory. Tricyclic antidepressants, most commonly imipramine, and the monamine oxidase inhibitors (MAOIs) are also sometimes prescribed, when the phobia is thought to be connected to an underlying depression, which might dissipate with such medication (see, for example, Stone, 1980, pp. 284–5). Occasionally, when more serious underlying pathology is suspected and the phobia is thought to be serving as a defense against its emergence, antipsychotic medication may be considered appropriate as prophylactic against further decompensation into schizophrenia.

Before discussing the case of Nadine, let me make clear that, at base, my philosophy is pragmatic. Many nonmedical psychotherapists take issue with, or are uncomfortable with, the use of medications; many who are psychodynamically-oriented reject the behavioral perspective. I do not oppose any of these treatments per se. On the contrary, I would recommend each (or a combination) of them in many instances, and have done so. The reader will note that, in fact, some in vivo work is included in Nadine's treatment, just as it is often combined with some systematic desensitization.

However, the case of Nadine is also typical of a particular kind of generalized phobia, one closer to the sort described by Kohut. The underlying factors may be classically Freudian, being rooted in the oedipal conflict, but more significantly, the expression of these factors in panic is due to "a structural deficiency of the self," caused by "the failure of the

oedipal selfobject milieu" (Kohut, 1984, p. 30). The root issue
may be, and in this case is, sexual and aggressive – or, as
Salzman (1980, p. 107) points out, it might be *"any* 'out-of-
control' impulses that would be a threat to the integrity of
the individual," such as "tender impulses, power drives, or
the need to maintain pride and self-esteem."

Kohut (1984) posits that:

> "it is the faulty responsive *paternal* selfobject that
> accounts for the first aspect of the structural disease
> of the self (i.e., the ascendancy of an Oedipus com-
> plex) and the second aspect (i.e., the patient's ten-
> dency to become overwhelmed by panic rather than
> being able to control her anxiety so it can serve as a
> signal). The mother, in other words, was apparently
> not able to provide a calming selfobject milieu for
> the little girl which, via optimal failures, would have
> been transmuted into self-soothing structures capa-
> ble of preventing the spread of anxiety." (pp. 29–30,
> italics his)

Through what Kohut calls *transmuting internalization*,
which is ideally fostered by some experience with "optimal
frustration," "the developing child has the opportunity to
take over the selfobject's function, to empathize with himself, so to speak, and is not too traumatized or upset to do
so" (Auerbach, 1985, p. 744). In fact, when we look more
closely at Freud's (1939, p. 74) hypotheses, we note that he
added a third category, of "aetiological traumas," that of "early injuries to the ego (narcissistic mortifications)."

Thus, the case of the patient presenting with a generalized phobia, from which no specific traumatizing event is
obvious, would be considered, as in the following case example, as one in which sexual and/or aggressive impulses of the
oedipal period may be significant, and in which characterological damage relating to narcissistic injury should also be
suspected. Where such injury exists, hypno-play therapy is

appropriate and often powerful. The therapist provides the very environment that was lacking. Such a "second childhood" makes it possible for the patient to internalize the "calming selfobject milieu" that is prophylactic against panic.

The use of auxiliary, secondary (but sometimes immediate) measures for symptom reduction is never discounted, however, but is employed for early relief. Whenever possible it is also important to prevent or reduce rigidification of a pathological family system adjustment. Whatever is done to ameliorate the symptoms helps further the positive therapeutic relationship in which the in-depth characterological repair work can eventually proceed.

As a hypnotherapist I am often asked to work with people suffering from phobias. Some referrals come from colleagues who think of hypnosis as a likely treatment of choice, being familiar with the literature of behavioral systematic desensitization, which often includes hypnosis in its protocols. More often, however, phobic patients come self-referred, having heard from friends of other phobia cases in which successful outcomes have been attained. This pattern of self-referral via other patients is particularly common when dealing with illness that the patient views as behavioral. Further impetus towards treatment is stimulated when the patient can no longer hide what has become a disability. Phobia cures are more likely to become public knowledge than those involving most other neurotic issues.

The existence of a seriously abusive and/or neglectful history lurking behind a façade of competence is always worth suspecting in cases where symptoms are severe. In recent years therapists have learned to attend to the almost silent signs of child abuse, incest, parental alcohol and drug addiction, and other previously underreported conditions lurking behind adult dysfunction. The child without a childhood cannot become a full adult, no matter how good he or she manages to look. A second chance at childhood is the logical treatment.

Nadine contacted me after hearing my name connected

with the successful treatment of an highly visible executive in the corporation in which she was employed as a secretary.

NADINE: AN APPARENT PHOBIA

> "If I had a choice of getting in an airplane that I knew would blow up 15 seconds after takeoff, or re-living my childhood, I'd get into the airplane."

An attractive, well-groomed woman of 42, Nadine had the tailored look of an upper-echelon corporate executive. She presented her problem in an articulate, appropriately direct, and affectively present manner. Labeling her condition agoraphobia, she cited the symptoms of avoidance of being alone in places where help might not be available in the event of a panic attack. Nadine's specific complaints centered around her phobias of heights, of bridges, and of driving: Within the agoraphobic milieu, the acrophobia seemed central, in that her fears of driving were especially focused around hills, particularly those from which vistas might loom up without warning. Similarly, her fear of bridges, including highway overpasses, seemed to have no association to the presence of water, but rather to the distance to the ground and the openness of the air around her.

Having been in what she found to be helpful insight-oriented therapy for three and a half years a decade earlier, Nadine was already acclimatized to the basic "rules" of therapy, was not excessively anxious in the session, and expressed her favorable view of psychotherapy and her hope for success with her problem. Her previous therapist, whom she had recently consulted, had discounted the need for further psychotherapy, suggesting that all that was required was repeated exposure to the feared situation. Nadine found that advice unhelpful considering her worsening condition, and therefore sought me out on a results-oriented basis.

Nadine traced the history of the phobia(s) to the beginning of her first marriage, identifying the initial panic attack as occurring during her honeymoon. A severe recurrence virtually incapacitated her immediately after the birth of her first child; attributing that attack to "allergy" to the anesthesia, she did not seek psychological assistance and gradually returned to partial functioning after several months without treatment. One further attack, at the funeral of her maternal grandmother, led her to request the assistance of a psychiatrist who prescribed Valium, which she took for only a few days, fearing the feeling of "loss of control."

After that time recurrences were sufficiently infrequent that Nadine did not find the symptoms seriously inhibiting until the year before her divorce, several years after the conclusion of her first term of psychotherapy. The phobic feelings were further exacerbated during the year of her alcoholic father's death, coinciding with her second marriage to a widower with children of his own. Nadine's mother, who had abused Nadine sexually and violently during her childhood, was still living. Their relationship was one of stable disengagement, with contact once or twice a year.

Despite recurrent panic attacks, Nadine still attempted to put herself in what she felt as threatening situations, such as accompanying her family on skiing trips. More and more, however, she was succumbing to avoidance, leading to participation in fewer recreational activities with her family and reduced opportunities at her job. At the time of her beginning therapy with me, even small inclines were becoming difficult, leading to complicated scenarios surrounding trips as small as neighborhood excursions to the supermarket. She recognized that the trend towards becoming critically incapacitated was accelerating.

As a firm believer that everything of importance is present in the first interview (though wisdom, as we know all too well, is most obvious in retrospect), I now note that Nadine made two affectively loaded statements during that initial session, both related to dependency needs: At one point, she exclaimed passionately, "You get fed up with being the strong one!" And, at the very end of the interview, she expressed anger at her previous therapist who, by refusing to acknowledge Nadine's need to work on the phobia in therapy, "wouldn't let me be dependent on her." The following factors seemed significant: a history of an abusive mother and an alcoholic father (the "better" parent); the occasion of the first panic attack (her first honeymoon); and the three events after which the phobia dramatically worsened (the birth of the first child, the death of the mother's mother, and the intersection of the second marriage and the death of her father). Given this data, as a first order (private) interpretation, I hypothesized that oedipal issues would likely be important and intertwined with insufficient and toxic parenting. Adding Nadine's criticism of her first therapist, I also suspected that dependency needs would be central in Nadine's therapy. Lacking a reliable selfobject, Nadine would require the bolstering or, perhaps, the entire construction of such a relationship from which, via "transmuting internalization" of the supportive, soothing parent, her sense of self-safety could be developed.

Considering the phobic patient's need to begin work with attention to the stated "problem," and noting that Nadine's current family structure was beginning to reorient towards support of her self-limiting adaptation, I began immediately with a direct attack on the phobic symptoms. In outline form, I constructed the treatment plan as follows:

1. Behavioral intervention
   A. Basic training in hypnosis
   B. *In vivo* practice driving.
      Simultaneous testing of hypothesis that support will lessen phobic reactions.
2. Psychotherapy in the office
   A. Historical material with attention to feelings about both mother and father. Investigation, understanding, labeling, and resolution of oedipal and other issues, as handled in previous therapy.
   B. Current family issues, with attention to family patterns related to phobic adaptations, secondary gains, marital relationship, problems around

      "blended family" conflicts. Possibility of seeing part or all of the family if necessary.

C. Revivification of early traumas, with working-through in trance and in conscious state. Attention especially to transference development.

D. Hypno-play therapy around early traumas.

E. Hypno-play therapy around incomplete and/or undeveloped stages of childhood.

F. Integration into adult coping mechanisms, including excursions into further or repetitive *in vivo* practice to test out any residual anxiety that may be surfacing in regard to issues that appear to have been completed or that are looming in anticipation of termination.

G. Termination

The very next week I started introductory training in hypnosis, followed by in vivo car rides in which Nadine drove with me beside her along a moderately hilly highway and over small bridges. Noticing immediate improvement from Nadine's point of view, which could be interpreted as a form of transference cure, I hypothesized that the linkage of "maternal" support—the Winnicottian envelope—enhanced by the use of trance (see Chapter 3) was an effective direction for the time being. Before any internalization could be expected, the mother-in-residence would have to be present in a concrete sense. At this early stage in the relationship we would not yet be dealing with the highly charged transference that could be expected to develop later. From a relatively straightforward participation in the events of symptom reduction, this partnership would lay the groundwork for further, more intrapsychic therapeutic work in which the transference would be central.

Thus, during the first phase of Nadine's psychotherapy, my role could be seen from two perspectives: On the one hand, Nadine perceived me as the "helping professional" whose pragmatic and supportive procedures would be effective. On the other hand, subliminally she was feeling the presence of the mother (or, in Sullivan's nonsexist phrase, the mothering-one) whose support had been desperately needed but not forthcoming and thus never internalized, and/or as the protector against repressed, dangerous sexual/ aggressive desires.

As therapy continued I learned further details of Nadine's childhood. Finding Nadine severely physically abused and sexually stimulated by her mother from at least the age of two through early adolescence, the family physician had threatened to have the children removed from the home. Nadine illustrated her attempt to pull herself out of the morass of misery—the lower half of her body still immersed, however—in a drawing spontaneously made after a hypno-therapy session in which work centered around feelings in early latency (Figure 1).

Nadine recalled no intervention from her passive though mostly pleasant alcoholic father. Her current contacts with her mother, limited to holidays and birthdays, were fraught with tension and conflict, as she tried to be "forgiving" while recoiling with fear and loathing in her mother's presence. Anger at her father was denied; he was, after all, the "better" parent. She noted without particular affect, for example, that he could give up alcohol for Lent but not for her graduation or wedding. The idea that, sober or even drunk, he might have served as even a minimal support to her when she was helpless was totally out of her consciousness. It was clear to me at this point in the historical investigation that the oedipal issues had not been resolved and might need to be postponed until later in the treatment.

Hypnotherapy took three forms with Nadine:

(1) *Anxiety reduction for* in vivo *work*. A standard induction of the eye-fixation sort was employed, with general suggestions for body relaxation following eye closure (see Chapter 8). The inclusion of an extended progressive relaxation sequence could have augmented the process, but was not necessary to achieve a moderate degree of muscle tension relief. The conventional, highly structured walk down a set

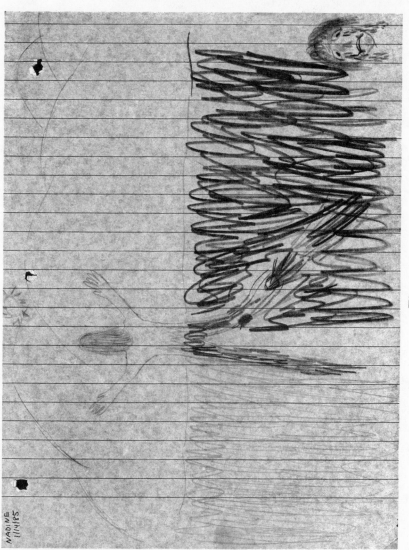

Figure 1

of ten stairs (see Chapter 8) followed relaxation. Despite the
acrophobia, Nadine showed no negative reaction to the
stairs; a path could have substituted if necessary. Arm levitation was induced after the walk, which terminated in a
"safe place" of Nadine's construction. During arm levitation
I introduced a posthypnotic suggestion, blended into a me-
lange of appropriate, symbolic fairy tales or animal stories
and, occasionally, songs created to support the theme of being held and safe. They simultaneously served to blur the
memory of the similarly contextually-designed posthypnotic
suggestion (see, for example, Lankton and Lankton, 1983,
pp. 218–219), such as one employed for the trip in the glass
elevator, described below.

(2) *Age regression for facilitation of early memory with
and without ancillary play therapy components.* In non-
directed age regression, a question or theme can be initially
set out, having been proposed either by the patient or therapist; or the therapist can facilitate a general search of various scenes at different ages in the patient's life until the
patient moves to focus on a particular scene from a specific
age (which may or may not be identified with adult clarity).
In the following example, Nadine had come to the session
having had an insight during the previous week: Returning
to work after an absence of a few days due to the flu, she had
felt insecure about her capacity to catch up. The phrase had
come to mind, "If mother doesn't love me, what good am I!"
The more she had thought about it, the more nauseated she
had become, feeling as if she might vomit. She came to therapy reluctantly, both wanting and dreading to know what
she felt was the question: When did my mother stop loving
me?

Nadine, by now an experienced hypnotic subject, went
into trance without formal induction as I repeated the question in her own words; she later described the experience as
being "like a white fog rolled up from here" (pointing to her
stomach). In the first segment of trance Nadine saw herself
bouncing up and down happily in her crib, making a lot of

noise. Mother entered the room. Nadine heard her humming, "buzzing back and forth"; Nadine felt more and more "scared." Seeing her mother approach, one hand raised, Nadine suddenly broke into consciousness, almost leaping off the couch, collapsing on it shaking and quivering.

After talking about the "memory," Nadine returned to trance. The next scene took her to the kitchen of her "old" house, where she had lived before the age of one. Unable to talk during trance, too young to have words, she made noises of choking and discomfort. In the conscious state she described the trance experience of being in a highchair. Mother "would just be mean," putting squash on a spoon and forcing it down her throat, making her gag. Continuing, she reported miscellaneous other scenes as they flashed by: of being on a changing table, her mother pinching her buttocks (a "sneaky meanness"); of being held, feeling "a warm fluid that was nice" in her mouth; of her left leg "pushing off" en route to standing up.

"When did mother stop loving me?" We considered the question again. By its very structure Nadine saw that she had felt that her mother *had*, in her experience, once loved her or, more accurately, that as a child she had once felt loved. In trance she had experienced a potpourri of scenes which, rearranged, give us Nadine's felt history: Held and fed as an infant, she had been satisfied. Over the next year, encompassing the visualizations of being diapered on a changing table and being fed strained baby food, there were at least incidents of felt abuse. Learning to stand up appeared without much affect: Nadine said she had sensed that her father was there but commented that perhaps that had just been her wish. By about 18 months we have the sheer terror with which the trance began.

From that point on, with all of the typical, and here exaggerated, issues of control that attend the toddler years, the abuse crescendoed into violence of newspaper headline quality. Intermingled with enemas were slappings and beatings which mother mentions today in adult conversation with no sense of their inappropriateness. Nadine consciously recalled building a shrine in the woods when she was 5, where she would pray to the Virgin Mary to intercede. When things did not improve, she concluded that her mother was more powerful than even the Virgin Mary, abandoning all hope for help at that point.

(3) *Hypno-play therapy for reconstructive purposes.* After the initial *in vivo* practice, in which Nadine was the driver, I took Nadine on walks and car rides (in which I drove) in the immediate neighborhood, preceding each trip with an induction and age regression to ages between two and five. Imagine any trip to the store with a child of those ages – with very little difference, you are accurately picturing an afternoon such as we would spend. Somewhat restrained at first, Nadine was a very "good" child, not touching the items in the stores without my explicit encouragement, never pestering for candy or little toys, which I would buy her with great enthusiasm. Eventually, she began to be swept up into my energy – I would exclaim, "Look at that!" and after a while she would begin to "catch" the animation and allow her own body and voice to take it in. As I would laugh at the antics of the animals in the pet shop, her smiles would grow into giggles. Even clerks, at first wary in their uncertainty, fell into the spirit of the childish fun; one such clerk, after falling into a gale of laughter himself, asked, "Do you guys have some kind of game going?" Sometime during the excursion I would just "feel like" having an ice cream cone and Nadine's appetite would perk up as well. One's dignity disappears with chocolate ice cream a-drip!

As might be expected, going "home" to the office was a painful trip. On the first excursion, during the drive back, Nadine began to tremble and cry. Feeling about three or four years old, she was able to tell me that Mommy would be mad because she had had a good time, and that Mommy would hit her. I remember feeling genuinely protective – the therapist in collaborative trance – as I said, "I won't let anybody hurt you." In the office, in that state which is some combination of trance and conscious adulthood, she revealed the felt rule of her childhood: "If you have a good time, you're going to pay for it." Learning to trust that no one would hurt her for having the audacity to enjoy life became the theme around which the successful outcome of psychotherapy was based.

All of the later reconstructive hypno-play therapy was based on that theme of the safety of having a good time. All future *in vivo* work, including trips to an elegant shopping mall to ride the escalator and rides up the glass elevators of Boston hotels, included aspects of "play" done in trance to whatever was the felt age, sometimes at preschool, sometimes at latency, sometimes at adolescent level. We bought souvenirs, such as charms she would wear around her neck, postcards – whatever spontaneously *felt good*. Fear of feeling good, with its previous expected price, began to fade, eventually disappearing entirely.

By April, just five months after beginning therapy, Nadine braved an airplane trip, using trance on the airplane, about which she was mildly phobic, to go to Disney World with her family. I received a postcard with the following text from her:

> I've never had so much *fun*! I'm doing it *all*, & loving *every* second. It's a Small World – Thunder Mountain – Peter Pan's Flight – Pirates of the Caribbean – the H-a-u-n-t-e-d Mansion (I loved it). We went to EPCOT yesterday and into Spaceship Earth – I'm so glad I did it – it was fantastic!! We ate dinner in "France" and as we were leaving late at night as we were looking up at Spaceship Earth all lit up I started to cry. I had the best day of my life & didn't want to go home. We all threw pennies in the fountain and made a wish!!

Noticing the childlike quality of the content and even of the vocabulary, it seemed entirely in kind that Nadine had forgotten to sign her name. Like a young school-girl, perhaps

six, she had the touching sense that her name was unnecessary with her "mommy."

Let the reader not be lulled into imagining that psychotherapy could proceed in this manner without movement
backwards as well as forwards. Between the successes, such
as a trip with her husband to San Francisco with hotel
rooms on a high floor and the endless steep hills to traverse,
were occasional panic attacks when driving alone on local
highways. When these would occur, Nadine would "talk to
herself," unconsciously introjecting my presence as she reminded herself that the panic was masking a thought she
had repressed. She would talk out loud, as if she were in my
office, and inevitably come to an insight, such as the realization that "it's not the height, it's being trapped with no support." She reported that the result of such a discovery was a
wave of relief, after which she would find herself smiling,
continuing on her way with a new lightness. The internalization of my "mothering" selfobject continued to grow; faced
with a moment of depression, she reported, "When I needed
comfort I thought of you. I could call you and ask if you
care, but I knew that, I had the feeling, and I didn't have to
call."

There were, of course, the inevitable resistances: "I don't
want to get over these things – I'm not big enough for the
outside world yet," Nadine proclaimed, procrastinating before the trip to the glass elevator. I agreed that no one should
have to grow up before being ready to do so, and that there
was all the time in the world to be a little girl. Surely she was
at last entitled to a childhood! Aligning myself with the
health in her resistance to grow up, I simultaneously expressed confidence in her capacity to do so at her own pace.
It was only a few weeks more before we took that trip, again
preceded by a hypnotic session in which further development of the theme of her introjection of my maternal being
was symbolically represented, with stories and images about
colors enfolding her in a cape of warmth and safety that
could appear whenever her unconscious was aware of the
need for it. "Forgetting" the details of that trance, Nadine

adapted that suggestion into yet another selfobject internalization: She told me that as she ascended the glass elevator,
"I thought of a rainbow coming into my heart."

It was not until the final phase of therapy that Nadine
dealt the mortal blow to her denial of her feelings towards
her father. By then capable of such directness, Nadine began
one session by announcing, "I think it's about time I dealt
with the issue of my father." At a dance that weekend she
had heard the song, "Daddy's Little Girl," felt tears in her
eyes, and promptly consumed five highballs. Shocked at her
behavior, as she had not felt like drinking more than a glass
or two of wine for over a year, she had allowed herself to
move past the firm denial that had been in place. She understood the resistance to that lifting of the denial: "Who'd
want it to come up – it leaves you totally alone!" She connected her insight to the agoraphobia and acrophobia: "That's
why all those open spaces terrify me – I had *nothing*, just
me." The total lack of support of either parent had been the
tragedy she would not allow herself to face. Now she was
strong enough to face the emptiness.

Considering herself a likable little girl ("I wasn't an awful
brat or something!"), Nadine felt her own righteous anger:
"How dare they not love a little girl like that!" Partially in
trance, partially consciously, she recalled scenes of her father's absence. Mixing her tenses, as in trance, she said, "I
can remember the lump [in the throat] and the hollowness. I
can be five, six, or a teenager." The nonlinear order of her
recollections did not perturb her, as she noted that "You
connect the *feelings*, not the ages" (what hypnotherapists
term the "affect bridge"). There was a resignation inside the
pain of those times, when neighbors would substitute for the
absent father at school or church events. As she put it, "It's
easier now that it's out in the open – it's like a sigh of relief. I
always had to say something good [about my parents], to
twist and turn to make it that way."

Recognizing the power of her father's alcoholism and of
her identification with him Nadine vowed, "I won't let that
make *me* drink, that could be the pattern." At the end of the

session, she told me her intention to give me a watercolor to which she had been so attached that she had carried a reduced Xerox of it in her wallet: It was the painting of a sad little girl, with whom she had identified. She felt that she did not need to carry her anymore, to remind her of the sad self inside that so few people knew. "I want to find a home for her—she should be with you. She has years to go to absorb all the fun." Giving it to me, she left that part of her in a symbolic union with her adoptive mother, while the free Nadine could finally go out and live.

Termination was a combination of retrospection and a claiming of Nadine's personal power as an adult. With the sadness came an understanding of the role that I had played with her: "Home is here. When I run home, it's here. . . . It's like you've known me since I was a little girl. With F. (her best friend), I *tell* about my childhood. You were there. You were there when you said you would be." Simultaneously, there arose acceptance of the damage caused by fear of being abused. Feeling a twinge of panic while driving, Nadine found herself saying aloud, "Roads don't hurt people; people hurt people."

Realizing that she was physically afraid of her brother, who had a history of alcoholism and abusiveness and who had recently threatened her with violence, Nadine concluded that she would register for a course in karate: "When we terminate, I'll have to pack my own parachute," she declared. In two months she has passed the tests for three belts beyond the beginning white-belt phase. Feeling physically safe must be her prerequisite for living. Like so many other clients, termination was expressed in vitality: "I want to live. I never had the momentum before." Surely this is what is meant by the transactional analysts who say that "Our Child is our source of creative energy" (Levin, 1974, p. 17).

As we concluded, Nadine worked out her own unique solutions. She imagined that after death, "If there is a hereafter, *then* I can let down and love her [mother]." "I don't have to deny that she's my mother," she added, "I don't have to deny the wish (for a mother), but I don't have to subject myself to the reality." She described her feelings about her mother as "a sad acceptance . . . , not a horrendous anguish," "a sadness with softness." Taking a Monday holiday to drive some 50 miles with me to Cape Cod, going over the Bourne bridge, back and forth some dozen times, she rejoiced in feeling "solid" on the highways, actually reveling in the view from the highest point, eventually becoming "bored" with the exercise. Impatient to live a full life, she applied and was accepted for a more challenging job with a future about which she need not be afraid. As she stated, "It doesn't have to work out . . . [the point is having] the freedom to try it."

Nadine has terminated knowing that a phobic response is one with which her body is all too familiar, and which might, therefore, recur under stress. However, the thought of such an occurrence no longer can reduce her options, because, as she explained it, "When I break the chains in my mind, the body follows." Thus she can be confident and excited about her life.

The above case is an example of the possibility of the felicitous interplay of behavioral, intrapsychic, and hypno-play therapy. The characterological damage done to Nadine in her early years had not been repaired by her earlier psychotherapy, which was focused on anamnestic discussion and current marital issues. There is no doubt that this former psychotherapy was highly useful, enabling Nadine to end an unsatisfying marriage and choose an appropriate partner, to understand and appreciate the severity of deprivation and abuse she had endured, and to construct for herself a life in which she had many satisfactions. The first therapy was not a purely intellectualized experience; indeed, Nadine reports abreactive moments surrounding the physical abuse which were at least partially worked through. Nevertheless, the important area of the capacity to feel safe in the universe was not significantly touched, because it was not handled on the young age level(s) at which it was basically lacking. Hypno-play therapy was essential in the completion of that work.

8

FROM INDUCTION TO EXIT: CREATING THE CONTEXT

Induction, for most hypnotherapists, is simply the way to arrive at trance state. Efficiency is the priority, and hence the ideal induction method is seen as that which will best forward the process. From this view, typified by Zilbergeld (1986, p. 107), long inductions are often considered a "waste of time"; the point is "to get to the therapeutic questions or suggestions." This approach suits some therapists, and doubtless works best for them. And that point is important: Whether the therapist admits it or not, a large part of the equation is personal style and experience; the needs of the patient as a particular individual and the specific goals of the trance are the other two factors significant in choosing the type of induction.

I view induction as part of the work of psychotherapy in general, and of trance in particular. In fact, I firmly believe that a good deal of successful psychotherapy takes place in spontaneous trance state, in which the natural rhythms of both parties have fallen into sync, perhaps, as Rossi (1982) proposes, with the coincidence of the ultradian cycles of both parties. The experienced subject, such as Bill (see Chapter 5) says, "When I hear your voice, I just fade out." Just as is often true in daydreaming, even the patient who has never been hypnotized (the so-called "naive subject") will glaze over, one hand perhaps numb and suspended, in the midst of some inner search.

As far back as 1931, Ferenczi (1980b) reported the appearance of such unintentional trance states – complete with age regressions – in many of his patients. His colleagues pointed out the similarity of free association, as he practiced it, to hypnosis, and Ferenczi, considering their opinions valid, conceded the point, henceforth terming that state "auto-hypnosis." Even more dramatically, some patients, such as Helen (see Chapter 10) retreat into what Kluft (1985, p. 203) calls "autohypnotic withdrawal"; During a session Helen's speech would suddenly slow, her head nod, and she would say, "I'm in a fog"; she would become "sleepy," close her eyes, and begin recounting scenes of age regressions or dreamlike sequences. No wonder, then, when I first encountered a demonstration of formal hypnosis, I exclaimed, "Ah, this is what I've been doing all these years – I just didn't know it!"

We have established that *formal* induction is not always necessary in the attainment of trance state; in fact, for the so-called "unhypnotizable," a direct induction may, as Barber (1980, p. 6) notes, be counterproductive. In the controversy about hypnotizability, I tend towards the Ericksonian stance that, since trance is a natural state experienced in everyday living, virtually no one is unhypnotizable. Time after time the myth of the unhypnotizability of certain types of people, such as those diagnosed in the psychotic range, has been debunked (Scagnelli-Jobsis, 1982). Many people, however – in my experience, perhaps 20% – resist the set formulae of conventional induction. Therefore, it is certainly advantageous to have some tools beyond the standard armamentarium with which to streamline the entrance process when trance does not occur spontaneously within the session. What is more, especially when dealing with age regressions, providing a formal entrance and exit facilitates the ability of patients to reorient to the world to which they will be emerging and in which they are expected to perform competently.

Thus, we will proceed to a discussion of induction techniques particularly appropriate to age regression and hypno-
play therapy; we will leave the core segment of hypno-play
therapy itself to Chapter 9. No epistemology of induction
will be offered. This approach will be simple and pragmatic,
emanating primarily from a combination of the therapist's
own past experience and the experience with the patient in
the moment. The induction, whether formal or informal,
whether direct or indirect, more or less permissive, will be
considered integral to the entire process of regression in particular and hypnotherapy in general. When one embarks on
an automobile trip, the specific choice of car, the time allot-
ted, the route, the itinerary are all important components of
the total undertaking. Having arrived is just one aspect of
traveling.

The journey of trance is one in which two people are involved, and the needs of both, as well as the destination, are
important. Both must be comfortable in the vehicle; each
will take a turn at the wheel. There must be provision for rest
stops, sufficient flexibility to handle the unexpected, the
leeway to slow down when desirable, and the possibility for
spontaneity so that one can take advantage of situations
that occur within the larger overview.

This chapter urges a practical and heuristic view of induction design for age regression and hypno-play therapy. Although some prototypical outlines for inductions will be presented, including moveable modules for particular purposes,
the reader is encouraged to create variations according to a
personal sense of self and style and, starting from that position, to develop protocols that will lend themselves to modi-
fication and problem-solving with patients in his or her practice. For the sake of simplicity the basic model will consist of
a standard, relatively direct induction, based on the commonly used eye-fixation method—originally employed by
Braid (Weitzenhoffer, 1957, p. 259)—which is still reliably
effective with a large percentage of people. In addition to its
simplicity, this method has the virtue of capitalizing on the
familiar experience of retinal fatigue, thus emphasizing the

natural, biological aspect of the hypnotic process. It seems best to eschew the use of objects such as pendulums or crystals, avoiding the magical connotations most lay people associate with hypnosis. Instead, the patient selects a target at which to gaze or the therapist provides a simple self-adhesive dot affixed to a wall (see Chapter 10).

Some patients have particular needs calling for nonstandard induction methods. For those unsuited or unresponsive to eye fixation, the therapist's sensitivity, creativity and familiarity with indirect approaches, as in the work of Erickson, will be necessary, and cannot, in some sense, be represented in recipe form. There are special requirements for nonverbal inductions, for totally nonvisual inductions (as for the blind), for rapid inductions (as in some situations involving pain control), for open-eyed inductions (with paranoid people, for example), and so forth. These adaptations are detailed effectively in courses offered by the American Society for Clinical Hypnosis and the Society for Clinical and Experimental Hypnosis. A sampling of books with many varied models of inductions include those by Pratt, Wood, and Alman (1984); Erickson, Hershman, and Secter (1981); Dowd and Healy (1986); Wester and Smith (1976); Erickson and Rossi (1981); Lankton and Lankton (1983); Weitzenhoffer (1957); and Brown and Fromm (1986).

While studying the following model inductions, the reader might find it helpful to visualize being in the office with a particular patient for whom hypno-play therapy might be effective, experimenting with the possibilities through conscious role-playing, of both the therapist and the patient, writing down or taping responses as they occur. Performing this exercise in light trance can enhance the fluidity of the therapist's own access to such potential data. Playing out the scene with another person, perhaps another therapist who would assume the role of the particular patient, can serve as valuable follow-up, giving the reader more experience before actually initiating trance for the first time with the patient. Optional alternatives are noted in parentheses in the Process column.

PROTOTYPICAL INDUCTION

Process	*Comments*
(1) *Introduction*: How pleasant it is to choose a position in which you feel comfortable, any position at all, (sitting up or lying down) (that's right) shifting your body until it says that it is feeling more and more comfortable in the chair (sofa).	Starting with *you*, in the cs* mode. The word *shifting* also connotes the cs/ucs movement. The use of *it* from now on helps to develop the split between cs and ucs and to encourage the ucs to emerge as dominant.
(1a) *Relaxation (optional segment)*: You might like to become aware of the feeling of relaxation as it spreads through your body, feeling each muscle relax, the day's tensions flowing out . . . your toes – relax; your ankles – relax (naming each body part, moving upward) . . . your face: your mouth, your nose, your cheeks, your eyes, your eyebrows, your forehead, smooth and relaxed, all the parts of your head inside and out, relaxed.	The Jacobson (1938) progressive relaxation sequence can be part of an induction, especially for the psychotic person with porous boundaries (Sands, 1986), for the physically tense person, or for the pain patient. In (1a) the "tensing" component is omitted.

The selection of the spot on which the patient will be asked to focus in the next section is relatively unimportant. As mentioned before, many therapists provide self-adhesive dots (available at any stationery supply store) affixed to convenient areas (just above eye level) in the office. The provision of such a dot is, undeniably, a directive element. It is chosen for a dual practical value: (1) Through offering such an object, the therapist is empathic with the anxious or obsessive patient, helping to reduce his or her rumination around the choice of a target. In that way the patient is relieved of the requirement to find a personal focus point,

*cs=conscious; ucs=unconscious.

although the freedom to do so is made explicit. (2) For patients who intend to practice self-hypnosis, duplicate dots, supplied by the therapist, do double duty as cues for post-hypnotic suggestion and as transitional objects. For greater flexibility in the practice of self-hypnosis, an anytime-anywhere attitude can be encouraged by having the patient select a target point on his or her own body, such as a ring or the nail of a finger. During arm levitation, dissociation, which "is a return to . . . early levels of functioning" (Erickson and Rossi, 1981, p. 241) will also be understood.

(2) *Eye focus*:

Now you can focus on the orange dot (or, any pre-chosen focus point; or, as you find yourself noticing a particular point on which to focus); the dot will seem to blur, and float . . . , your eyes getting tired . . . , your eyes getting irritated (comment on physical manifestations of such irritation, such as tearing) your eyes telling you that they want to rest, that they want to close, heavier and heavier . . . (When eyes close you can add, for greater effect, a sequence in which the patient will then open his/her eyes, allowing them to close "when they want to"; and/or, for even stronger effect, a sequence of the Spiegel (1972) eye roll – though note that this method is inappropriate for headache sufferers, whose symptoms may be aggravated by it.)

Still some attachment to the cs. More or less directive style. If P. is anxious, add explanation of retinal fatigue.

Shift to ucs mode by assigning personification to a body part, creating a dissociation especially useful with patients who are unaware of their body feelings. T.'s voice gets slower, deeper, softer. Pace breathing to match P.'s.

Any of a number of techniques can now be inserted for what is generally termed *deepening*: A progressive relaxation module, if omitted earlier as (1a), can now be introduced,

especially for patients with physical tension with or without
specific body pain, such as neck and back spasms; the patients can be repeatedly brought in and out of trance (*frac-
tionation*); images in which the conscious and the unconscious are separated more and more widely can be employed
(see, for example, Lankton and Lankton, 1983, p. 143ff);
metaphoric stories can be interwoven in an Ericksonian combination of symbolic and confusional techniques (see, for
example, Lankton and Lankton, 1983; Zeig, 1982, 1985a, b,
c; Erickson, Rossi, and Rossi, 1976); and/or a simple, relatively linear procedural regression through time can be employed through images evoking numbers. In an especially
permissive method, advocated by Rossi (1986), the patient's
unconscious makes the total decision for or against deepening, signaling via eye closure or ideomotor response (see the
case of Miriam, Chapter 4). Many hypnotherapists make use
of hallucinated calendars, the pages turning backward (or
forward, in age progressions) in time; however, I prefer the
staircase image, which lends itself to more involvement of
the body. Although many hypnotherapists count upwards,
the movement from 10 to 1 seems more congruent with the
concept of deepening and emotional grounding; thus, I take
the downward direction. As the patient fantasizes moving
down the steps, more possibilities multiply for kinesthetic
sensation along with those of smell, hearing, sight, and, with
some imagination, even taste. For patients phobic of
heights, a path along which they can walk, still "step by
step," can easily be substituted.

(3) *Staircase*: And you might find it interesting to allow yourself to create a staircase of 10 steps (or, you might find yourself thinking about a staircase; or you might find yourself standing at the top of a staircase).

Equivalent images can be created with numbers, using elevators, escalators. Take care to avoid phobias. By using *might*, *interesting*, and *allow*, the therapist is being permis-sive and encouraging creativity. One might also be directive: "Imagine a staircase . . . " when permissiveness breeds too much anxiety for the patient.

I wonder what kind of staircase it might be? . . . What kind of wood . . . or perhaps some other material . . . what the surface is made of . . . you might take off your shoes and socks, and feel the texture, perhaps a smooth floor, or perhaps a carpet, or rubber treads . . . and the feel of the banister . . . the colors . . . As we go down . . . 10 . . . 9 . . . and the sound of your feet . . . 8 . . . and the temperature on your skin . . . the taste of the air . . . 7 . . . your eyes so comfortably closed, feeling heavier and heavier (or calmer) with every step . . . 6 . . . and every breath . . . slower, deeper . . . so interesting, you can almost smell the colors . . . 5 . . . relaxed, and comfortable . . . and feel the sounds, the shapes and forms, the tones of textures in your body . . . 4 . . . and your body may notice details it has never before known, one hand just a little heavier than the other . . . with every breath, heavier and more relaxed, holding more and more of the conscious concerns . . . 3 . . . as your other hand becomes freer, lighter . . . I wonder if you can see a bunch of helium balloons floating by, all the party colors (can add details if patient is not visual) their long strings reaching down, attaching to the lighter hand, feeling the tug up – up – lighter and lighter . . . 2 . . . a little breeze under the fingers . . . 1 . . . float . . . such a lovely feeling . . .

Therapist goes with patient by using we.

Avoid "heavy" with overweight patients.

Synesthesia, a cross-over of different senses, is both a creative and confusional device.

More dissociation.

Beginning of catalepsy. May be done during staircase sequence or after last step.

Using a lighter voice. Both for ratification of trance, and as a metaphor for the putting aside (not the elimination) of the defenses, the use of catalepsy is important. When necessary, the therapist can lift the patient's hand the first time, leaving it suspended and then pushing it down to allow it to rise on its own.

The use of catalepsy for anesthesia/analgesia, for promotion of amnesia, and for deepening and ratification of trance state is a common device in hypnosis (Erickson and Rossi, 1981, pp. 56–57, 194–195). In addition to these functions, catalepsy can serve a symbolic purpose. As the patient's hand floats, it represents the very possibility of "letting go" of the usual defenses which keep him or her bound to conscious considerations. Yet, the other hand, by comparison and suggestion feels so heavy that it cannot be raised from the lap. By this method, while letting go, the patient is still grounded, and thus partly anchored in the real world. For those who are particularly anxious about abandoning their defenses, even for a brief time, the therapist can create the scenario in which the grounded hand is holding the defenses or coping mechanisms temporarily, as one might shift one's shopping bag or attaché case to one hand in order to free the other in holding the strap of a bus or, for a younger image, in holding the hand of another person. Additionally, the therapist can suggest that the patient's legs are also becoming heavy with the weight of the defenses. All comments made here are, of course, intended merely as starting places for the sensitivity and imagination of the therapist, who will constantly be monitoring and reappraising the situation and the responses emanating from it.

(4) *Lovely place*: And as you continue to float, you can find yourself approaching a lovely place, just the right place to come to rest (arm may lower or not) and you see there just the right chair to sit in, a chaise lounge, perhaps, comfortable and relaxing. Your body knows . . . just right for you. And you look around, and see a beautiful place, exactly what your body needs (can add details, as with the staircase) . . .

It may be convenient to encourage the arm to lower, because it may be necessary to use it later.

(5) *Screen* (Occasionally omitted for experienced subjects who move directly into the hypnotic work):
And there, in front of you, you find a screen, a movie screen, or perhaps a television screen. You have a remote control in your hand, with an on-off button and some other buttons that you may choose to use. And as you watch, the title of the movie appears on the screen: JOHN (name of patient). It is a movie about you, when you were a little boy (girl). But no one has put it in order, all the ages are mixed up, so many scenes. And you can watch them now. Perhaps you will want to stop the movie – put it in pause – take a long look at some particular scene. Or you might like to turn the volume up or down. And I'm sitting next to you. Can you see me there? (Wait for nod or other signal.) Can you tell me what's happening on the screen?

The screen is a conventional technique to foster age-regression with the choice of distance from the event left to the viewer. Control is firmly in the hand (literally) of the patient. P. can be directed to specific ages of many scenes "if your ucs finds this an appropriate time and place to do this work," when the goal is work around a specific traumatic incident, or reconstruction of a specific period.

Here the therapist has the opportunity to assess the age of the patient. Ideomotor signaling, which is generally limited to yes/no/don't know/maybe responses, can be used if the patient does not talk. But it is definitely preferable for all efforts to be made to encourage at least some speech during trance, as the therapist's ability to evaluate the developmental level, as well as the particular experience of the patient, will be greatly enhanced by having access to more of the patient's inner world. Additionally and importantly, the therapist may feel greatly limited by the patient's silence when traumatic material is being abreacted. In that situation, using a method frequently employed by Erickson and Rossi (1979), the patient can be roused to the alert state for a discussion of the material, and then easily returned to trance for continuation.

(6) *Exploration of scenes*:
(P. describes scene, or, if necessary, ideomotor questioning continues. Therapist pulls for sensory details, notes if the patient shows any behavioral or language regression yet. If affect is important, T. can inquire if patient would like to know more about what is going on with little Johnny — can use child's name for him or herself. If not, move to another scene.)

Strengthening P.'s involvement.

(7) *Entrance into scene*:
(If yes:) And you can get up from your chair and go over to the screen. . . . Can you go all the way over to the screen? (Don't push if patient becomes panicky; in that case, do preliminary work with patient at some distance from the screen.) That's right . . . and you can even reach out and touch little Johnny (P.'s name), feel his little hand in yours . . . noticing your foot stepping into the screen . . . is it your right foot or your left foot? . . . And the other foot . . . and the rest of your body . . . and as you come closer to little Johnny (looking down at him; you may feel like hugging him) you can feel yourself getting smaller, moving into his body, your body, younger and smaller, just_____years old . . .

This process can be lengthened when especial difficulty with the material is expected. T. should be careful to support the wisdom of the patient's ucs for its caution.

P. can be at the back of a movie theatre, for example. Heightening physical involvement.

Movement into the scene.

At this point the session can proceed either to an investigation of a particular scene being remembered, with or without abreaction, or to the direct use of play therapy as a reconstructive modality, as will be detailed in Chapter 9. The use of time distortion to expand or contract the experience of revivification and/or reconstruction can easily be employed. As has been discussed in Chapter 4 and will be further discussed in Chapter 10, any traumatic material that is uncovered must be treated to some degree during the very session in which the uncovering is taking place. Best, of course, is the immediate application of reconstructive play therapy, after which such "remember/forget" instructions (see step 8 below) are optional (although always harmless) and dependent on the extent of the trauma and of the success of the play session. Exit stories which emphasize the theme of the play module and which offer metaphors encouraging introjection are especially effective in such situations. Post-trance discussion and interpretation in the adult state are an absolute imperative, although such may occur within the current session or in sessions subsequent to the trance work.

In the sample exit from trance below, the reader might imagine that the patient is a middle-aged man who has reexperienced a traumatic scene from his early life and who has had the opportunity to play around the troubling affect of that life event. Perhaps the therapist and he have been battering the cloth puppets as he was battered; perhaps they have been building and knocking down each other's blocks, discovering the nonlethality of destructiveness.

(8) *Exit*:
And now you can begin to feel
your body move apart from
little Johnny's body — your legs,
your torso, one of your arms —
it would be nice to hold one of
his hands just a little
longer . . . feeling yourself
getting taller once again,
older . . . he's just a little

boy... because it's time to go
for today ... something sad
about that ... but you can say
goodbye, you can come back
and visit him again. .... And
letting go of his hand you find
yourself moving back through
the screen, to your lovely place,
finding that special comfortable
chair. I wonder if you've
pressed the remote control yet,
or whether the film is just
running on to its completion as
you can settle back into that
chair, your eyes closing peace-
fully... remembering the
staircase we will be going up
again ... 1 ... 2 ... (begin
telling stories, adding safety
feature of being able to forget,
to forget to remember to forget,
as the unconscious knows what
we (it) need(s) to know when we
(it) wakes up ...) 3 ... 4 ...
5 ... 6 ... 7 ... the eyes becoming lighter (finish story by
8) ... beginning to flutter
(whenever they do) ... 9 ...
arousing slowly, comfortably
... feeling refreshed and
alert ... 10.

Emphasis is placed on completion, on acceptance of feelings
of loss.

Important to reverse process in
its entirety, reaffirming P.'s
control over the process. In the
trance phenomenon, where P.'s
reactions are concrete, any
omissions are felt as disquieting.
The *we* can include the therapist as part of the unit if
desired.

T.'s voice getting lighter, pace a
little quicker.

THE OPTION OF AMNESIA

At the very least, should play therapy and/or waking interpretation be impossible due to time or other restrictions,
it is imperative that the revivified trauma be covered afterwards by trance instructions which allow patients to "forget"
any material that his or her unconscious deems inappropriate for the conscious to be aware of at the current time.
As Hilgard (1966, p. 106) has noted, spontaneous amnesia is
far "less frequent than suggested amnesia," so one should not

count on doing nothing as satisfactory. A sandwich method for structuring amnesia, in which the material to be forgotten is set between relevant but distracting material, has been developed by the Lanktons (1983) and is admirably detailed in their book (see, for example, pp. 218–219). In this regard it is particularly useful for the therapist to tell stories on healing themes as part of the climb back up the stairs. It is also possible that the therapist may see value in prescribing temporary recall amnesia, so as, theoretically, to evade the patient's powerful defensive set which might, in its well-practiced resistance, keep the patient on the old track longer than necessary. Lastly, when the therapist thinks that the patient will likely resist any input that does not feel as though it comes completely from the inside, the therapist might prescribe what Evans and Thorn (1963) call "source amnesia," in which the patient recalls what has occurred in trance (e.g., the therapist's story), but recalls it merely as a familiar tale rather than as one authored by the therapist.

Whatever the mode of arriving at the place at which play therapy can be effected, one must take into account the previous trance experiences of the patient, the degree of trust already established in the therapy situation, the personality structure of the patient, and the type of material that is expected to emerge (with due humility for human inability to anticipate the surprises that often occur). As a general rule, the more anxious the patient, the slower and more protective should be the induction. Sensitive pacing can accommodate an extremely wide range of situations. As has been described in the literature (see, for example, Scagnelli-Jobsis, 1982), induction can be safely achieved even with patients whose excursions into psychosis are frequent; caution and careful planning are especially mandatory in such cases, where issues of intimacy and boundary permeability are paramount. For example, with Dick, a patient for whom I was not the primary therapist (see Chapter 10), an induction was safely conducted in the presence of both therapists; it took almost two hours to reach the point of age regression, by using the imagery of a large theatre in which the patient could move at his own pace, step by step, to the screen. As contrasted with age regressions without hypno-play therapy, where the patient can obtain distance by viewing rather than becoming part of the scene if necessary, play therapy does involve the patient's participation at the age in question and is hence more literal and concrete.

THE SPECIAL CASE OF THE HYPNOTIC DREAM

Although hypnotic trance is not sleep, it is often associated with the sleep state or, more accurately, with the hypnagogic state that precedes actual sleep. In its lighter form, trance might be thought of as a free, extended daydream, a literal absent-mindedness with little awareness of the here-and-now. In its deeper state, although brain activity does not register as sleep, trance appears almost indistinguishable from the dream state. Thus, the marriage of dream work and hypnosis seems almost ineluctable.

There are many scenarios from which to begin: Sacerdote (1967) details a variety of options. But the therapist needs only a few basic ones in order to custom-tailor work with dreams in trance:

(1) *Work to complete an unfinished dream.* The patient presents a dream that was interrupted by internal process or outside interference. The patient enters trance with the intention of completing the dream. The therapist can repeat the dream to the patient in the patient's own words, which have been noted exactly, or an audiotape of the recitation of the dream can be played. The patient is instructed to re-dream the dream through to its conclusion, reporting the details in real time or after the completion. If the patient reports it while dreaming, the therapist can remain predominantly silent, with an occasional "mmhm" to indicate attentiveness, or the therapist can participate in the dream, asking questions and/or adding details and direction, in that

way influencing the result. The latter, of course, is perfectly legitimate as part of psychotherapy, but should be recognized for what it is, a participatory shared construct.

(2) *Trance to produce a new dream, for expansion of the work in the session.* The aim of this option is the investigation of a particular problem or issue or the explication of another dream. In this situation, the therapist instructs the patient accordingly, restating the question or issue when the patient has reached trance state. Again, the dream can be left totally to the dreamer or can be a cooperative effort between patient and therapist.

Inductions for dream production are basically no different from those for age regression, with the exception, perhaps, of more emphasis on "sleep." When appropriate, of course, informal induction is always an option. For a more standardized induction, the therapist might suggest the supine position and offer the patient pillow and blanket. In reference to the previous protocol, steps 1 through 3 would remain unmodified; catalepsy usually enhances the development of the dream state. One can make use of catalepsy itself as an ideomotor signal by linking it to the dream production: "And as you dream, your dreaming hand can float comfortably along with that dream, settling back in your lap as the dream comes to its conclusion . . . " The dream work might then proceed as follows:

T: Floating, drifting . . . and your unconscious can reclaim your dream of last night (tell dream in patient's own words). And then . . . (Or, you can find yourself in your dream world, and you can have a dream that can in some way help us to understand the issue/dream that has been keeping itself outside your consciousness.)

If dream was interrupted by P.'s process, rather than by an external source, there may be strong affect and/or resistance, requiring T. support.

One would then work with those dreams according to the material that emerged, using play therapy if appropriate. The therapist would then continue through the prototypical process as previously presented, making sensitive adjustments reflecting the material that has been produced in the trance in the usual manner.

Does experience show certain types of dreams to be most appropriate to hypnotherapy in general? To play therapy in particular? There are no hard and fast rules on which to lean, although there are a few directional arrows. One of these is, of course, the presence of early material, that is material whose manifest content involves childhood or whose theme reflects early issues that the therapist recognizes as especially cogent in the patient. For example, I do not pursue Bill's dream (Chapter 9) by using hypnosis. Since the issues of that dream are ones that arose primarily late in Bill's childhood, becoming particularly prominent in adolescence, it was more fitting to deal with that dream in a conscious, psychodynamic formulation at a later point in the session.

Second, a hypnotic approach seems especially valuable when the usual free-associational methods have produced relatively sterile results, especially when the patient can think of "nothing" to talk about in relation to what appears to be a symbolic dream production. A hypnotic investigation can almost always be used with a patient appropriate for hypnotherapy as adjunctive to free association.

Additionally, the use of hypnosis does not rule out other techniques. Gestalt dialogues, for example, with or without a play therapy component, are often particularly appropriate both for dream analysis and for reworking of scenes revivified during age regression. Whatever methods the therapist may wish to employ can often be incorporated into the hypnotic envelope with highly potentiated effects.

This chapter has addressed the nuts and bolts of induction, with a focus on age regression into which a unit of hypno-play therapy can be appropriately inserted (see Chapter 9). But nuts and bolts are just that—hardware necessary to the creation of a structure, but not to its essential design or meaning. The reader holds the possibilities for significant work in every encounter. The art of therapy can never be taught, but only rediscovered in the spirit of exploration, imagination, and responsibility.

9

USING PLAY THERAPY
IN TRANCE

Long before I became aware of hypnosis as a discipline, I interned at a clinic that was, like many, somewhat short of office space. In the round robin of room assignments I occasionally found myself scheduled to meet with an adult patient in the playroom. It was hard to miss the longing expressions of some of these adults as they eyed the toys on the shelves or "helpfully" – and infinitely slowly – replaced a stuffed animal left on the floor by the previous occupant. It was second nature to begin to incorporate these materials in the environment into the adult "talking therapy" sessions. The more primitive the developmental level of the patient, the more useful these sessions seemed, and I began to request the playroom for particular patients.

After the conclusion of my internship, the next few years led me to more traditional office environments, and I failed to recognize the importance of what I had accidentally learned until I began private practice. Then, due to the ages of my own children, various toys remained in a basket in a corner of the room which I had converted to office space. Thus, the discovery of the use of play therapy with adults was twice serendipitous; remaining in my unconscious storehouse of knowledge, it remained to be refound and reworked with the additional momentum of the power of hypnosis to fuel it.

136

THE WAITING ROOM

The waiting room is the ideal place in which to introduce materials which beckon the playful involvement of the patient. Looking for something to do, patients search for items to engage their interest, distractions from anxiety. If all that is available is the very magazine just read at home, the desperate will pick up even that. Why, then, settle for the ubiquitous magazine rack, when the therapist can offer such temptations as a magnetic sculpture to be teased into ever-original shapes? In my experience even the most rigid of people cannot resist the lure of this toy. And how about crystal prisms and various kinds of kaleidoscopes? Those who peek through them, must by definition notice — again with appropriate symbolic value — that the world looks different when viewed through various lenses, that the same components can create totally new and intriguing pictures when shaken up. In addition to the obligatory hanging plants, the office and waiting room areas can display some easily accessible seedlings whose progress can be easily monitored and appreciated both in concrete and symbolic ways. Moreover, in the bookcases of learned tomes Freud can rub shoulders with Dr. Seuss.

THE OFFICE

One need not abandon all conventional office furnishings — chairs, couch, lamps, tables, perhaps desk — to make allowance for improvisation. However, in addition to these staples one can expand one's definition of "the office" in many creative directions. Being a musician, it is natural for me to include musical instruments in my office, vehicles by which to experiment with sound, to express the unsayable in melody and rhythm. It is often advantageous to include a piano, whether full-sized or table-top keyboard; playing together with a "child," improvising songs which serve to express repressed affect or humor, represents another "way in" to the often untouched, virgin territory from which new growth can spring. In essence, the therapist's imagination (and, of course, the physical constraints of the office itself) is the only limitation, once the therapist takes the attitude that adult and adult-child play experiences have intrinsic value.

In a visually separate area of the office one can locate the young corner. Adult patients will doubtless notice this area, though conventional self-restraint will inhibit them from approaching it without invitation. Research has indicated that play therapy is generally found to be most effective under the age of 12. But, as Lebo (1956) points out, that fact may well stem from experience with adolescents, who disdain and distance themselves from children's toys, although, in fact, they might enjoy them. Erikson (1951) noticed, for example, that Harvard-Radcliffe students were resistant to playing with the toys offered to them. Once covered by a rationale and a specific task (to build a dramatic scene with children's blocks), however, they set forth, appearing to be "overcome by a kind of infantile excitement which . . . could be shown to have originated in *childhood traumata* . . . ." (p. 669, italics his).

First, then, the therapist accepts the adult's initial resistance to the idea of playing with children's toys by informally dividing the child and adult areas. But by designing both areas to be visible simultaneously, the implication is made that regression is, in fact, a separate experience that exists within the context of wholeness. The boundary between here-and-now and early work remains intact. However, through the existence of the adult toys there is tacit approval for the translation of the feelings of childhood into current life. Respect is thus offered for the external adult and for the child within.

Most of the materials provided for the adult "child" are similar to those conventionally supplied for the chronological child in play therapy environments. When choosing items, remember that, as Stern (1985, pp. 166–167) had observed, even children as young as 18 months use such materials as dolls with symbolic intent. The young corner can include table and chairs; art materials; Play Doh; children's books; a xylophone; a pounding board and hammers; a dart board; a large box of wooden blocks of various sizes, shapes, and colors; an erector set with tools; large and small balls; mitten puppets; masks; water or soap bubble guns; beads; string; hammer and pegs; cars and trucks; wooden and bendable "people" of different races, ages and occupations; soft animals; baby dolls of both sexes; balls; a bop-bag; play food; nursing bottles; dinnerware for little "parties"; a few simple games such as Chinese checkers; and an assortment of interesting "junk" — bottlecaps, sequins, costume jewelry, matchbox cars, and so forth. A doll house can be useful; however, most are solid structures which do not lend themselves to rearrangement. What is the child of a housing project to make of a colonial edifice! Blocks, on the other hand, have the advantage of serving to build whatever house is in the patient's mind. It is nice to be able to offer water and sand as well; if the therapist finds it impractical to provide such messy materials on the premises, trips to the local playground can supplement the available resources. Art items should also be limited to those that the therapist can handle without undo anxiety about the condition of the room and the clothing of both participants.

THE USE OF VIDEOTAPING

The hypnotherapist might also consider an investment in a video recorder and camera. Involvement in the hypnotherapy relationship is a full involvement, sometimes including some extent of mutual regression. Certainly, hypno-play therapy requires the therapist's near-total immersion in the hypnotic agenda with the patient. Especially given the current lack of structured workshop training in hypno-play therapy, it is immeasurably advantageous for the therapist to be able to view the session afterwards, for self-observation, as well as for supervision with one's consultant and/or peers. Moreover, there are times when watching the tape together with the patient may be of particular importance, as patients begin to integrate their early growth into adult life.

One brief caution: Taping is not an end in itself. Therefore, the equipment should be as automatic and non-intrusive as the latest technology can provide. As the therapist is likely to be working without an assistant, filming can be done from only one observation point and therefore is limited to a single camera. Therefore, the camera should be provided with automatic focus and a wide-angle lens. Lighting should be adequate for all hours that the office will be in use; the built-in light meters on most cameras will inform the novice if the lighting is sufficient. The video camera can be mounted on a tripod with wheels to facilitate mobility; or, as a more expensive solution, it can be mounted on a swivel base built onto a shelf attached to a wall. A long, heavy-duty extension cord for a tripod setup extends its flexibility. Multiple external battery-powered microphones are far superior to the camera's condenser microphone; by means of V-connectors and extension cords, two or more microphones can be arranged near or attached to the therapist and the patient for optimal acoustic clarity.

The camera novice need not take flight at what may sound like a plethora of paraphernalia requiring sophisticated technical knowledge. Lacking other informal resources, about 15 minutes of on-site instruction from one's local camera supplier will suffice to prepare the rank amateur for the successful operation of a complete video apparatus. During any therapy session, the time taken to arrange such properly situated equipment effectively will be limited to about one minute, the time required to insert the tape in the video machine, attach the microphones, and press the ON button. Anyone who can operate a television set has all the qualifications needed to film in video.

DESIGNING THE PLAY MODULE

The more passive forms of play therapy do not require particular attention here, since the therapist's technical problems are minimal. Increasing depth of trance can be attained through a number of conventional methods or simply by assigning deepening to the physiological response the patient is emitting (e.g., "with every sigh you can go deeper. . . ."). When sufficient depth is reached, the play activity is introduced. In other words, at that point, while the patient is in trance, the therapist can read to the patient, recite a story or poem, sing a song, direct the patient to look at the lights reflecting from a prism, offer a stuffed animal to stroke, or whatever. If it is necessary for the patient's eyes to be open for the activity, one simply makes that request ("and you can find it comfortable to open your eyes now . . . ").

If the use of either of the patient's hands is necessary for participation, one will utilize the hand that is not cataleptic. If the use of the dominant hand is required, however, previous care is best taken to assign the nondominant hand for catalepsy. If that opportunity has gone by unattended, do not despair: Simply add an instruction for the cataleptic hand to lower. That behavior could perhaps be linked to another desirable accomplishment such as that of eye-opening ("as your right hand begins to lower you can find yourself moving even deeper into trance, your eyes finding a way to open as your hand touches your lap . . . "). Where only one arm is necessary, a levitation reversal can be effected for the same deepening result ("as your right hand begins to lower, how interesting to notice your left hand getting lighter and lighter [in appropriate voice], that set of helium balloons [if you used that image] attaching to the wrist of the left hand, floating up, up, giving your right hand its time to rest, resting on your lap . . . ").

The tape excerpt below illustrates the use of stuffed animals in a hypno-play module. Being a relatively simple procedure requiring no large-scale deviation from the typical practice of age regression, this example might serve as a good introduction for the reader's initial entrance into this specialty.

MADELEINE: USING STUFFED ANIMALS

Madeleine, a painter in her twenties, spent a good deal of her childhood traveling among homes in Europe, due to her father's work. She identified the theme of "going away" as fundamental in her life, finding those words coming to her mind frequently. Trance was induced with the prototypical method, the patient lying down as she preferred. I suggested a screen on which some image might appear that would shed light on the identified theme. It is interesting that Madeleine's vocabulary in the conscious state (not reproduced), in contrast to her speech in trance, is exceptionally erudite and scholarly.

P: I'm seeing the maid, the family maid, while I was very young, her name was Thea, and she had a very big chest, very soft, and black hair, and I mostly think about her chest, how soft it is, and being held against it [mm]. I really want to be with her (cries).

Note the shifts back and forth from past to present tenses.

T: You miss her.

P: Yes, I do, and she's gone, she has to go away.

T: Why does she have to?

P: I don't know (looks confused).

P. seemed very young, as if my questions made no sense.

T: How old are you?

P: I don't know. I have little white boots on (sobs).

T: You're really feeling so bad.

P: I want her to come back! EE-YA! (In a very plaintive small voice) She's much nicer than my mother.

(Child's pronunciation of Thea)

T: Can you make her come back?

P: No, she's gone forever. (In a more adult voice) I think she went to Greece. (In a younger voice again) *We're* staying and *she's* going away. I can say her name as much as I want and it doesn't help. She does everything . . . [compares to mother who is demanding and restrictive].

Notice that, as Hilgard (1977, p.46) comments, "the observing ego . . . when present . . . need not interfere with the vividness of the regressed experience."

T: You're just a *little* girl.

P: (In older voice) I'm feeling like you're my mother now, Marian, smaller and more tight inside . . . not so soft.

Boundaries are blurring between Thea, mother, and me.

T: You'd rather have Thea, it's safer with Thea.

P: Yes, it's really great. . . . I don't want to eat by myself.

T: Does Thea make you do it?

P: No! She feeds me! (crying quietly) I want to say over and over—EE-Ah. EE-Ah. (In an older voice) I think it's her last day in the house. I think I see her suitcase. She's dressed up in real clothes, not a uniform. (In a younger voice) I want to find her. I want to go where she went. (Cries, then begins to reconstitute)

An interpretation of P's yearning could have been made here, or can be saved for the conscious part of the session.

T: Do you know how old you are?

P: Somewhere less than two, but I don't *know*, I know from

reading and asking. (Lies on the couch looking desolate)

T: (Getting several stuffed toys and a rag doll) I have a whole bunch of friends who'd like to hug you, your chest looks so lonely. (P. hugs all of them to her.)

P: (Looking at the doll) I don't like her, but I'd like to get to know her.

T: She had a hard life, that's why she wears long dresses, she doesn't want her body to show.

P: (Noticing that doll has no demarcated mouth) And she doesn't talk.

T: What would she be saying if she had a mouth?

P: AAH! (disgusted sound)

P. has issues about her body and sexuality. Sexual abuse during childhood has been suspected.

The above is an example of a relatively simple logistics problem: All that is needed is for the therapist to get up and fetch the toys to be used, placing them in the patient's hands. But how could one get the patient to walk over to the toy area if that were necessary while still in trance? It is possible. As the sleepwalker navigates stairs in nocturnal trance state, so can the patient in a somnambulistic condition. When the patient's eyes are open, they can see. The patient can even take a walk with the therapist outside the office, although one had best hold an arm while crossing streets; naturally, the therapist must take full responsibility for the hypnotized person as one would for a young child.

In the office, once the patient's eyes are open, there is no difficulty with any play activity, be it playing patty-cake, building towers of blocks, banging on a drum, painting, drawing, shooting water pistols, composing a puppet play or opera together, sculpting with clay and sand—the therapist's imagination and expertise with chronological children are the only limits.

If trance should lighten, the therapist can opt to deepen it or can suggest that the patient do so, as often as necessary during the session. On the other hand, the therapist may prefer to take advantage of the patient's growing willingness to participate in play activity in a more conscious, nearer-adult mode.

As when doing play therapy with chronological children, the hypno-play therapist must have in mind a specific goal, using play to introduce and develop it, sometimes within a single session, sometimes over several sessions. In the above example, the goal was the exploration of the patient's difficulties with loss in her adult life. The secondary issue of sexual abuse emerged, as traumatic material often does from the experience of having opened the door to memory within a safe and supportive environment. To that end, as with children, the therapist usually takes a nondirective, permissive attitude, waiting for the patient to "experience growth under the most favorable conditions" (Axline, 1964, p. 35). Or, when relevant, the therapist can move to a more active stance, as in the case of Barbara (below), especially when there is a deficit in experience in playing. In such cases with chronological children, as Irwin (1983) points out, it is appropriate that "the adult is the child's first play companion and tutor. . . ." (p. 167).

BARBARA: BUILDING ANIMATION
THROUGH PLAY WITH BLOCKS

Imagine, in the following example, that the patient is Barbara, the depressed woman in her forties introduced in Chapter 6. You have observed that she has had a joyless, grey life in which initiative has been squelched; due to other evidence, you speculate that she has great anxiety about expressing anger. In this session (whose transcript, due to long periods of nonverbal play, has been telescoped from two hours into one), as is typical for her, she does not move

spontaneously towards any of the available toys. You therefore decide to use an active approach. In pre-play therapy
trance, Barbara has given you the feel of being about three
or four years old, based on her vocabulary.

T: Oh! Here's the block box.
What a lot of blocks! Want to
look with me? (P. looks in,
passively.)

T. takes initiative, adapting
vocabulary to preschool level,
sounding enthusiastic enough
for two.

T: (Puts hand in box, messes
around, making noise with the
blocks) What a lot of blocks!
Here (taking P.'s hand), do you
want to feel them? (P. puts
hand in box, moving it around
gingerly.)

T. must lead the way.
Best to include as many
sensory modalities as possible.

T: That's right. Oh, that sounds
good! Can I do that with you?
(P. begins to move her hand
around in the box more
vigorously, nodding. T. and P.
get into sync, making more and
more noise with the blocks.)

Joining P. in the activity makes
the activity escalate while the
patient remains safe.

T: How about we DUMP ALL
the blocks on the floor! What a
big noise that will make! (T.
and P. upturn the block box
with a loud crash.) AAAH!!! (P.
smiles tentatively.)

Or, a game could be made of
pitching each block out of the
box, if T. feels that dumping
would be too big a shock at this
point. T. must still carry the
ball, making most of the noise.

T: Ooh – look what I've got
here – a door! What's that red
one there (that P. was looking
at or touching).

P: A window!

T: A door and a window! And
here's some people. Here's a
little boy with no hair! (laughing)

The message is: Silliness is OK.

P: That's funny! (Touching the
doll's head, smiling with
amusement)

Therapist and patient go on to build a house together, adding matchbox cars, a little train, whatever. They make up a story together.

P: Here's the Mommy. Where should she go?

T: I don't know, what do you think?

Since P. is now really participating, T. takes secondary part. Note that P. is taking care of Mommy. Mommy's fear of abandonment may be an issue.

P: Mommy can stay outside. Here's Auntie. (Puts "Auntie" next to Mommy) They can talk to each other.

T: Now Mommy will be happy. (P. gives vigorous nod.) What will we do now?

P: Put Grandma in the house. Making cookies.

After this daring behavior, it is important to stress partnership with P.

Play continues, in which the doll children have more and more fun, while Mommy and Auntie (who remains a sort of Mommy-sitter without distinct personality) remain on the sidelines. T. and P. begin to build towers with other blocks, adding to the scene. Sometimes a block falls — it is especially interesting to note that P. attempts to balance blocks with the naivete of the small child. Modeling task-centered concentration, T. sometimes works on her own tower. At other times, shifting to a cooperative mode, T. participates in adding blocks to P.'s tower. Crashes dominate, and laughter ensues more spontaneously. As the session moves towards greater freedom of physical and verbal movement, T. introduces the risky issue of the acceptability of anger by initiating a small "play fight," with words chosen for their double value:

T: You knocked my block off! Oh, now I'm MAD (said in a joking voice). I'm going to knock your block off too!

The attempt here is to decondition P.'s fear of her own anger and of the anger of others.

P: (Giggles) I'll knock your whole tower down. (She does.)

T: Who cares, I'll make another one! And I'm going to use this truck to deliver the poles.

The options are open to develop the fight or to end it creatively. Keeping the goals in mind, and the developmental gap being addressed, either (or some other) choice is made.

Play continues, with mini car crashes and crescendoing sound effects until the end of that segment of the session, when both T. and P. clean up the blocks by pitching them into the box.

When the play segment or module is complete, the therapist takes the patient back to the "adult" area of the room where the return to the "pleasant place" is effected (step 8 of the prototypical induction). A posthypnotic suggestion can be embedded during the walk back up the staircase. For the above example, one could consider such a suggestion as, "You will be able to notice a new delight in familiar sounds," or "You may find yourself laughing at nothing at all," or "You may surprise yourself by enjoying the thought of something silly." One suggestion is as much as a patient can absorb. Any particularly threatening affect—in the above example, anger—warrants a cautious approach during the embedding process. Here, for example, one would not choose to embed a suggestion about feeling angry or feeling comfortable with anger in an out-of-office experience until an in-office conscious adult experience has been successfully negotiated.

Although trance has been formally terminated, the therapist must remember that some elements of that state remain for a few minutes. The therapist can attend to this extension of some degree of light hypnosis by being alert to the dominance of the patient's use of single-syllable words (Shapiro, 1977). While emerging into adult awareness (the length of words increasing, the vocabulary becoming more adult), the patient is encouraged to talk about the experience, to become aware of the new feelings of relaxation and pleasure in the adult body. Some interpretation or observation of the play therapy might be made. For Barbara, the therapist might comment, "You are very careful not to leave your mother all alone." Often there is discussion of the issue brought up, here the patient's role as the parentified child, her view of her responsibilities, her image of her mother as somehow helpless, lonely, fragile. At the end of the session, the patient might want to walk over to the young corner and look at the toys again, or even to hold one or two in her hand. With Barbara, it was especially valuable to use adult "toys" or attractive objects, such as the kaleidoscopes nearby, as transitions to the adult world.

On nice days I might walk Barbara to her car, examining the flowers by the side of the path – touching, smelling them en route. We would also occasionally take out-of-session walks as "two adults," when I was free to do so. Such walks were part of my regular daily routine, and Barbara's company was not burdensome; in fact, as she became more and more affectively present and animated, this activity became increasingly pleasant. These walks served to smooth the transition from patient to nonpatient and to incorporate the goals of the play-therapy segments into a way of living in the world.

BILL: THE THERAPIST AS PEER

We have seen the therapist as adult therapist with "child" patient (Madeleine), and as parent with "child" (Barbara). A third role for the hypno-play therapist is that of peer in the play-therapy life of the child. With the "older" child, especially, it is common to find the patient alternating between past and present while in trance. Thus, the therapist, who by age is most frequently more peer than parent, almost naturally can assume the role of child-peer with such a patient. In the example below, the edited transcript is of a one-hour hypno-play therapy session with Bill, who was first seen in Chapter 5. The play segment grew out of the following comment made by Bill earlier in the session:

> I don't put a lot of faith in friends or whatever. [T: I'd
> like to hear more about that.] I've done without them
> for so long. . . . It can get you slapped around. . . .
> I'm the original chameleon. . . . They want the three-
> piece suit side, they get the three-piece suit side.

The reference to "so long," and the use of the strong verb
"slapped around," pointed towards the utility of an open-
ended age regression to a time that would "shed light" on the
issue. A brief excerpt from the beginning of the trance segment follows:

P: I'm on the street with Dora
Brown. She's nine.

T: How old are you?

P: I'm nine also. . . . I got a lot
of kidding. I like that girl Dora,
but I don't know how to talk to
her. In front of my house we
play truth/dare/consequences.
You choose one of the categories. They set me up 'cause they
know I like Dora, she doesn't
live around there, a couple
blocks away. They kept asking
me to ask her to go steady, but
I was afraid.

Switch to past tense
P. continues in past, T. continues in present. P. then returns
to present.

T: Can you ask her?

P: Naw, I'm chicken.

T: How do you feel?

P: Nervous, very bad. . . . I'm
small, I'm not cool. . . . I'm sort
of – there are dress fads, my
parents are a little conservative,
I wear regular corduroys,
Buster Brown shoes . . . the boy
next door, the one the parents
like . . . you're a safe bet.
They're right . . . boring! I'm
the littlest.

Notice the adult awareness of
the scene mixed with the child's
experience.

Connected both through affect and similarity of plot, Bill continued to talk about this and other scenes in which he felt humiliated and even betrayed by his peers, with girls, and in his attempt to be accepted in the school band. His size added to the feeling of inferiority and vulnerability. Eventually we reached adolescence, when the racial issue became more prominent:

T: Where are you?

P: In_____(a white suburban town), with Joan and her girlfriend. They have a (summer) place, we all packed up and went. I was the only Black person there. Learned to be a very funny fellow. . . . I looked at myself as the weekend entertainment . . .

P. vacillates between present and past tenses. Continues in past tense for a while.

T: How old are you?

P: 12 or 13.

T: Do you feel tense when you're there?

P: Not really – I'm in control . . . I think, all the world's a stage, keep 'em laughing. Even the biggest bigot in the world, they let their – um – tensions are gone, their resistance falls. . . .

T. Remains in present tense. It would seem normal for the one Black to feel under stress, and since stress and high blood pressure were presenting problems, T. is investigating the origin of his defense against it. Note that P. now remains in present tense for a while.

T: Do you want to go on this weekend?

P: Oh, sure, I get to go out on the rowboats, out in the ocean. . . . I listen to Bill Cosby records. . . . it depends on your delivery.

T: It works well.

P: You betcha.

T: So 12-year-old Billy knows how to do that, and nine-year-old Billy doesn't know too well.

P: It was boring to be me, to be short. To be funny, people listened to you. . . . I go to school with Sol, he's an artist; Kevin's my best friend, he plays basketball. I don't have a specialty, they're unique. . . . But I am funny, then they laugh with you.

Again, the vacillation between past and present.

T: And no one's laughing *at* you.

P: When you're the one making the jokes.

T: It hurts to be laughed at. The little boy is very smart, he learns how to stop the pain . . . He can't change that he's Black, and he can't change. . . . Maybe he can be funny if he practices it, and then be somebody special, and people won't laugh *at* him anymore. . . . How are you feeling right now?

T.'s interpretation is couched in young language.

P: Tired.

T: Why are you tired, Billy?

P: It's not fun to be funny all the time. . . . I'd like to be accepted just for me, not 'cause I'm funny, not 'cause I'm colored, not 'cause I'm anything, just because I'm me.

P. uses term *colored*, common during his childhood, one he never uses now. Note that earlier he had called himself Black, when speaking in the past tense.

Taking the theme of the desire to be "accepted . . . just because I'm me" as the yearning that, when thwarted, became covered by the defense against the danger of trusting, a segment of play therapy around that theme was introduced. Play therapy seemed particularly apt, as in earlier sessions Billy had spoken about his "fence walking" at his job as a "game" of "walking close to the edge without breaking my neck." Although that attitude kept him safe, he felt more and more "isolated" from his colleagues and, in comparing himself with others, said, "I know what it means to be a lonely person. I've been lonely 40 years of my life." In this case I therefore adopted the role of peer, to which I felt there would be least resistance, as many of Billy's playmates were white, and as his issues were mostly peer-oriented – white peer-oriented in particular. I began by setting the stage, moving from the past tense almost immediately, as I observed Bill slumping further into trance state:

T: You know, not too long ago I was a little girl, and I can see me nine years old – and I had braids . . . and striped shirts . . . and Indian Walk shoes. . . . I hate those shoes. . . . My mommy makes me wear them 'cause they're good for my feet . . . (P. going deeper into trance). You know, I like you a lot, you're a good kid. I don't tell on my friends. I won't tell on you if you won't tell on me. Do you want to be my friend?

Beginning in past as if using screen. Paralleling his description of his clothes and shoes, moving into present tense.

Reference is to his experience of betrayal.

P: Yes. (Nodding slowly)

T: I'll teach you to play skelly checkers (a street game with bottle caps) if you don't know how. You know how?

P: No.

T: (Describes game) What would you teach me?

P: Drums!

T: Would you teach me?

P: Sure!

T: We could be partners! Deal?
P: Deal.

A metaphor for the hypnotherapeutic relationship.

T: .... and when we come back
to this room we're really going
to play skelly checkers ... tell
you a secret, I got a good move
the other kids don't
know ... and you can stay in
trance if you want. .... (T. rises
and gets the skelly checkers. T.
sits down on the floor; P. joins
T. on the floor. T. gives P. a
skelly checker.) Here, you can
have one, because you're my
friend.

Anticipating a transition —
optional. I may have been
feeling unnecessarily anxious
about P.'s willingness to play,
given his elegant attire and
usual formal presentation.

P: Thank you! (T. demonstrates
how to shoot the checkers,
teaches P. the rules of the
game. T. and P. play for a
while.)

P: *They* want to play to win; I
want to play to play.

P. often avoided conflict and
competition, so T. models both
options.

T: Sometimes I want to play to
win, sometimes I want to play
to play.

P: (Nods acceptingly)

T: Isn't it nice to have a friend
and not put on an act, just be
you.

P: Yeah, not tiring.

Echoing his earlier sentiments,
T.'s tone indicated that T. was
speaking for herself, although
using the ambiguous "you."

Sessions of hypno-play therapy concluded with an almost
imperceptible return to the fully conscious state. Suggestions were made directly that Bill would construct a set of
skelly checkers and practice the "good move" he had been
taught. Bill followed these instructions with enthusiasm,
bringing the results to the next sessions.

The next weeks evoked more memories of the games of
latency through adolescent years — descriptions of mumble-

ty-peg ("I don't know why I thought of it!"), of friends of those eras, of playing board games with his father. An emergency surgery precipitated a dream about Fisk, which allowed Billy to appreciate the lack of tension around being part of an all-Black community:

> It was a long dream, about Fisk, a real tight camaraderie type of dream. I dreamt about being on campus, feeling the feelings of the football game. A homesy atmosphere—it hits you in the chest at football games. I felt like I was going to die—I wanted to say, if they knew what I know now they don't know how good they have it. I felt sad—it was like watching over it, going to the cafeteria, sitting with the guys. It was like I made the fucking trip! [T: What's the sadness about?] Leaving. My primary concerns were not what they are now, dying, being Black.

Billy also began to bring in dreams about repressed anger—a tame dog vs. a vicious bear, for example. The play-therapy trance was partially recalled, as we integrated reference to skelly checkers into the conscious sessions; however, much of the specifics of the hypnotic sessions remained "kinda hazy." Unlike Billy's usual discomfort with forgetting anything, he exhibited a *belle indifference* towards the forgotten details. But the power of that session emerged in his forceful new insight and focus:

> If people were circles, I'd be 3/4 of a circle. Someone else might say, "Where's the other part?" I know it isn't there. [T: What do you think the missing quarter is?] Being able to do what I do *here* anytime I choose to.

In continuing with Bill in psychotherapy, further work in both conscious and unconscious modes proved to be a constructive direction.

In this chapter the reader has been introduced to the use of hypno-play therapy as employed occasionally or frequently within a generally conventional psychodynamic framework. The set-up of the office implies correctly that this method is always an option to be chosen when appropriate. The above examples offered no particular difficulties; those in the following chapter represent cases in which the use of age regression is more fraught with complexity.

10

PROBLEMS IN THE PRACTICE
OF HYPNO-PLAY THERAPY

Hypnotherapy gives rise to certain problems in and of itself; adding the component of play to therapy with people whose bodies are those of adults increases one's problems geometrically. This chapter will concern itself primarily with issues that arise from the union of psychotherapy, hypnosis, and play therapy. We have already seen that the definition of play is nebulous and that differentiation between trance and consciousness includes a transitional fuzzy arena in which definitions eventually succumb to hand-waving. Similarly, the boundary between internal and external reality is to some degree theoretical, perhaps even artificial. Nevertheless, I will arbitrarily sort these problems into bins that may make them more intelligible for now. I urge the reader, however, to bravely allow the muddle of possible overlaps, logical loops, and multidimensional thinking to overtake linearity when reprocessing into a schema of thought and practice.

INTERNAL PROBLEMS

By *internal problems* I refer to those problems that occur because of the intrapsychic processes that are activated by the use of hypno-play therapy with adults. I include all aspects of transference and countertransference, with their powerful defenses of projection and projective identification. Because hypno-play therapy is not an entity unto itself, but

157

is ultimately a form of psychotherapy using hypnotic age regression, whatever the reader has learned and discovered about these processes is as true and as important as ever — and more so. Hypnosis is a state in which the relationship between therapist and patient is transsensual, rhythmic, intense, often primitive. It is stronger than the form of empathy that Kohut (1959, p. 463) terms "vicarious introspection." In regressive hypnotherapy the therapist cannot remain outside the envelope — and yet, to use another form of that word, must not become enveloped by it. There is no clear safety zone, no yellow line to stand behind. Good supervision or consultation around such cases is imperative. The following issues are particularly important.

Intense transference with some patients

Transference becomes extremely intense, often early in the course of treatment. Most commonly, this transference is positive, which is all to the good, as it seems as true for adult/children as for children that, as Anna Freud (1964, p. 37) noticed, "the positive transference . . . is the prerequisite for all later work," much more so "than in the case of adults." In particular, as many, such as Fromm (1968, p. 77), have noted, this transference reaction is one of "infantile dependency." The patient perceives the therapist as the good, omnipotent, magical parent, good often in the sense of the one who fulfills the felt deficit of childhood. The patient thus develops an idealizing transference, which often includes stimulation of dependency needs, leading to yearnings or demands for the therapist's time and even physical presence on a daily basis.

And, in fact, as Winnicott (1965a, for example) repeatedly reminds us, it is necessary, at this dependent stage, to be careful *not* to fail the patient. Patients with borderline or narcissistic disorders who have not yet developed a reliable sense of object constancy, often cannot evoke the memory of the therapist during the briefest of separations. To sustain themselves they will request a photograph of the therapist,

replay tape-recordings of sessions, or dial the therapist's telephone answering machine so as to hear the familiar voice.
On an even earlier developmental level, in which the out-of-
sight object is simply vanished totally from the face of the
earth, more terrifying fantasies hold the patient in their
grip.

For example, Helen (see below) marveled that a friend,
worried about the lateness of her husband, expressed that
concern as "Where can he be?" For Helen, there was no
"where" – someone who does not show up on time has simply
"disappeared," vaporized like a puff of smoke, gone to some
great beyond that is unimaginable, a place she called the
Land of the Lost, a phrase her mother had used to describe
the fate of missing keys, socks, and other trivial items. Such
a patient is in a state of terror daily, tortured by ordinary
comings and goings of life: the children leaving for school,
the spouse to work, and so forth. She *cannot* have a reliable
sense of the therapist, or of anyone else, as an internal or
even external object. While the adult part of that patient
would cognitively be able to appreciate the fact that separation from me did not mean my total and irrevocable evapora-
tion, the child part of the patient, as another patient put it,
would react to my unavailability by an internal "on-off
switch" which would result in total panic. *It is vital that the
therapist respect the needs of these patients as appropriate
to the patients' developmental level and as indicative of the
kind of attachment that is the seed for eventual mature relationships.*

If weekends feel unbearable and interminable to the patient during this early phase, vacations often are real crises.
Anticipating a three-week hiatus, Elaine (presented later)
who had already become able to keep me in mind for several
days at a time, put it clearly and poignantly:

> The thing that's been on my mind . . . there's still
> something that I'm terribly afraid of [T: mmhm] and
> all I can describe it to you as is that I'm just afraid of
> losing contact with you inside, of shutting you out,

of not caring . . . [T: And it feels like you can never
come back from there]. Not only does it feel like you
can never come back, there's another element to it,
that I'm a very bad person . . . and it's excru-
ciatingly painful to think of myself in those terms
when I *have* loved and cared about you so much and
you loved me and cared about me so much. It just—I
can't stand the thought of it.

Should the therapist set what seem to be the usual reasonable limits regarding extra-hour contact during ab-
sences, the patient will feel abandoned, often desperate, and
possibly suicidal. As Winnicott (1986) reminds us, "A child
who has not experienced preverbal care in terms of holding
and handling—human reliability—is a deprived child." Being, at heart, optimistic, he tells us that "To do it later in a
child's life is difficult, but at any rate we may try, as in the
provision of residential care" (pp. 147–8).

The outpatient hypno-play therapist is trying to do it
without residential placement, hoping to maximize the positive adaptations and good functioning. There are times when
it takes faith in the light at the end of the tunnel for both the
patient and the therapist—and even more so, of course, for
the patient, who is feeling the sense of starvation at every
deprivation of total care. As Helen (see case following) put it,
the terrible thing was the "grief" at having to go home at all.
Being relegated to a "slot," no matter how many times per
week or how long, was excruciating and enraging: "Schedules just do not work for me!" It felt unbearably painful to
her to feel that I might not be available, which would feel as
though I did not *want* her, retraumatizing her at the point of
the original fault.

Thus, the patient will complain in an unappreciative way,
leading the therapist who does not understand to feel manipulated by a spoiled brat, a complaint often voiced by hospital staff about their borderline patients. But the truth is not
that the patient is a spoiled brat, but that the patient is a
starving child. Nothing the therapist can do *will ever* be

enough, and the therapist had better understand that and be able to handle the consequent feelings when taking on such a case. Whether openly expressed or not, anger at the depriving therapist will be intense and unforgiving.

HELEN: NEED TO MAINTAIN CONTACT WITH THE THERAPIST

Helen, an attractive, intelligent woman in her thirties, sought therapy around marital problems and various phobias. She also evinced obsessional concerns around minor bodily complaints. Shortly after beginning therapy she began to regress spontaneously during sessions, revealing great deficits and deprivations extending throughout childhood. Her treatment consisted of a combination of hypno-play therapy and consciously-oriented psychodynamic psychotherapy. Since she had seriously lacked in nurturing during infancy, work centered around that period and included bottle-feeding, as is commonly practiced with "autistic children and others known to have suffered severe infantile deprivations" (Haworth and Keller, p. 331). A little later work expanded to investigation of the environment through sensory stimulation during walks, picking flowers, looking at shiny objects in stores, eating ice cream cones, touching different textures.

Therapy was interrupted for three weeks during a trip arranged many months previously, with dates fixed due to a conference. Although appointments were arranged with another therapist during the period of my absence, when regressed, the patient, although able to retain my image in her mind, could not use anything less than my concrete presence as a reality to which she could hold. Thus I anticipated that such a separation would feel like a death. Although the patient had audiotapes of the sessions, and could and did play them between sessions, I was concerned that doing so might reactivate the issues being addressed during the long absence triggering further regression.

To maintain the patient at a level of at least partial compensation, I arranged to telephone her at pre-set times and to send postcards at frequent intervals. As the country to which I was going had limited and unreliable telephone service, the patient needed to arrange to be at her telephone for several hours in order to be sure of receiving the call. The plan was difficult to carry out but did succeed, so that the patient was able to maintain adequate equilibrium, to remain compensated throughout, and to continue the regressive hypnotic work afterwards.

Therapists using hypno-play therapy must expect that their patients will have the difficulty described in Helen's case. Like the young victims of child abuse and neglect described by Mann and McDermott (1983, p. 304), these patients will first engender rescue fantasies in the therapist, feelings that "are often quickly shattered when the 'child' enters the regressive-dependent phase in therapy. Suddenly, the therapist may be overwhelmed by the demands for attention and nurturance which alternate with angry outbursts when the patient's needs cannot be met. Feelings of inadequacy, frustration, and hopelessness are then common." Such feelings are also frequent, as what may seem like an inconsequential behavior will be responded to as a gigantic error on the primitive level at which it is likely being experienced. The therapist must therefore carefully self-analyze all such events from a theoretical and a countertransferential view.

It is essential that therapists limit the number of cases at such a regressive phase, remembering that a commitment to a regressed patient includes hours that will feel like emergencies, and will drain the therapist accordingly. Similarly, as in the case of Elaine below, when "in the position comparable to that of a mother of a newborn baby," the therapist will suffer from "hate in the countertransference" similar to Winnicott's (1958h, pp. 201–202) impressive list of such hatreds which affect the normal mother. At the least, the therapist will often be suffering from intense anxiety, which may lead to apathy and withdrawal, what Sullivan (1953, pp. 57, 80) calls "somnambulistic detachment," producing the "evil nipple" of the anxious mother. In addition, when working at such a primitive level, the tendency of the therapist "to repeat or invert a certain infantile relationship with his parents in which he sacrifices either himself or them" (Racker, 1968, p. 177) is an especial hazard. No matter how "healthy" the therapist, when doing work of this sort any remnants of neurosis are bound to slither to the surface.

Thus, it pays to treat oneself carefully, to be closely attuned to one's own needs. The patient with very early dependency issues must be considered in a special category. A rough guide that I have found practical is to count one clinical hour with such a patient as equivalent to at least four standard clinical hours. That is, one should reserve those extra hours as time that could be given to the patient should that be necessary. One need not be unoccupied during that time—writing papers, doing administrative work, any activity which can be interrupted, would be suitable. Since it is likely that this needy patient will also be scheduled for at least four hours a week, one such person in treatment with hypno-play therapy is probably as much as a therapist can handle well, given perhaps 14 more hours of a continuing standard practice (assuming a 30-contact-hour week).

As would be expected, the issue of payment is especially difficult in such cases. The small child should not have to pay for parenting, and the adult small child feels the same way. Nevertheless, most therapists expect to be paid! Thus, issues of fee charged for extended telephone appointments, and for out-of-session contacts must be dealt with explicitly and must be resolved in a way that leaves the therapist feeling fairly compensated. The monetary arrangement that works with the least amount of painful interference in the process of early development is the best choice, given the therapist's personal orientation. Parenting with resentment is a noxious reexperiencing to be carefully avoided.

Intense countertransference related
to early issues and dependency

Countertransference becomes extremely intense, due to the therapist's own early issues and the real-life stimulation of feelings generated by the excessive dependency of the patient, which intrudes into the therapist's life. Issues of nurturance and lack thereof are common to those in the "helping professions," for whom taking care of others often serves as a substitute for a felt need for caretaking *by* others. Therapists with such issues run the risk of feeling caught up in, and/or resentful of, the amount of caretaking required by the hypno-play therapy patient. In addition, while doing this work, the therapist is not seen as a person — certainly not as a real, multidimensional human being. Rather, the therapist is sometimes almost literally an object from which gratification comes, a breast, so to speak; Greenbaum (1978, pp. 198–199) details such a case in which, becoming increasingly annoyed at requests for extra sessions and extra-analytic telephone intrusions he finally identifies his feeling of being "used — not as a person but almost as an inanimate . . . transitional object derivative." One patient, raging at the information that I would need to leave promptly at the end of a session, was explicit: "You're not a person, you're a therapist!" he shouted. In short, the therapist becomes annihilated, "deleted" (Erickson and Kubie, 1941, p. 592f), someone else in the patient's life. The therapist's own need to be recognized must be almost totally sacrificed in such a relationship.

Moreover, Lindner (1960, p. 66), among others, has wisely asked whether hypnotherapists, even more than conventional psychotherapists, choose their specialty out of a reaction formation: doing "good" rather than doing "bad." Such therapists run the risk of acting out during the likely occurrences of the patient's projective identification, thus repeating and exacerbating the damage already suffered by the patient. For those for whom grandiosity is a tendency and the experience of power a seductive magnet, it is all too easy to slip into acceptance of the patient's idealizing transference, creating, in Lindner's term, a "shared neurosis." It's hard to resist the pull of such expressions of love as those of Helen, whose cards would speak of me as "the most special person in the world." The smile of warmth such a note brings is real and is an important part of the relationship. The problem arises only when the therapist needs to believe the content as objectively true.

As Freud (1925) pointed out, by living out the role of the omnipotent god-like being, the hypnotherapist overcomes the threatening feeling of helplessness. The therapist is also at risk for developing the delusion of the saintly rescuer, again, to cite Freud, attaining in the community "the reputation of being a miracle worker." It is all too easy in such a setup to find oneself using the patient for one's own narcissistic gratification. And all of us are candidates for such a reaction. For, as Benedek (1959, p. 409) posits, parenthood is "a developmental phase" in which the child's fantasies reactivate in the parent the omnipotent fantasies of his own childhood," the period Ferenczi (1980, p. 219) so aptly termed that of "unconditional omnipotence." The therapist, ever flesh and blood, is thus also prone, in hypnotic parenthood, to the same stimulation.

The hypno-play therapist is often all too aware of the rapid erosion of personal life and space, as frequent telephone calls, common for some time with both Helen and Elaine, interrupt family time and as the pathetic, clingy "child" requires hours far beyond the typical comfort level of the therapist. The child's being an adult complicates matters even further, when family members, both adults and children, feel extruded by or jealous of the "competitor" who, to them, appears to be an adult, and yet is playing with child's toys, being taken for walks and ice cream cones, holding hands with *their* spouse in the street, and playing with *their* mommy or daddy in the sandbox. Dealing with the resulting family problems will add still more stress to the therapist's life.

ELAINE: DEMANDS ON THE THERAPIST'S OUTSIDE LIFE

A vigorous, physically fit middle-aged lawyer was being treated in hypno-play therapy for feelings of worthlessness which persisted despite her obvious brilliance and many wide-ranging talents and accomplishments. Belying her attractive, professional appearance embellished with hand-crafted jewelry, she obsessed about suicide almost daily, practiced self-mutilation under particular kinds of stress, had been injured in several accidents, and had made a direct suicidal attempt many years ago.

In her age regressions Elaine frequently returned to the preschool ages of approximately two to five. She wept, screamed, and withdrew during these regressions; issues of inconsistent parenting, of withdrawal and overinvolvement, emerged as a sense of her having been the victim of emotional battering within a framework of parental good intentions.

Elaine requested daily sessions of one and a half hours each; I was not able to accommodate more than three such sessions per week, two of an hour and a half, one of an hour. In addition to the in-session hypnotherapy I encouraged her to telephone me when she felt the need for additional contact; on off-days and on weekends she sometimes became so desperate that I was concerned that she would become actively suicidal. During and after this period I arranged to have the patient accompany me on Saturday errands, during which time the patient would maintain her adult compensation on an external level, although she reported that she felt uncomfortably "little" at the same time.

As Winnicott (1958, p. 297) notes, patients who need to regress to an early stage of dependency have an additional conundrum: they are aware of the situation, as the baby is not. Of course, those patients are often embarrassed, thinking back in the adult mode on childish behavior in the office or even in public.

More serious, these patients are probably frightened. Rose was one such woman, previously hospitalized for serious suicide attempts. In treatment with a colleague for over five years, she began hypnosis with him after he sought training in hypno-play therapy in the service of making progress beyond her "stuck" place. After eight sessions of age regression, she expressed her vulnerable position to him clearly: "I think, okay, I'm letting you in further, so if something goes wrong, it will hurt more deeply, it's gonna be more devastating than before when I was more careful and wouldn't let myself feel anything about you. . . . I'm at a higher risk now. I don't know what will happen. I don't know what I'll do." Suicidal acting-out was a very real possibility for Rose, for, as Winnicott (1965b, p.209) put it, such behavior "is the alternative to despair," of which there is no shortage. All therapists will find themselves under stress when dealing with the safety of a despairing patient whose inner resources are few and whose fragile equilibrium is being shaken. The therapist must not panic – and yet must not fall victim to denial of potential for tragic outcome. A fine line to walk indeed!

One need not, and should not, walk that line alone. Noticing my crescendoing levels of stress with patients in the regressed dependent stage, through such markers as physical tension and specific dreams, I take care to avail myself of consultation to make sure that my evaluation of the ongoing situation remains objective. Attending to my own needs for nurturance and diversion with family and friends becomes a priority during these periods and makes it possible to maintain a full involvement with the patient throughout each crisis.

As true for both Elaine and Helen, it is often necessary to invite extra-hours contact, as the patient has been trained long and well in feelings of worthlessness and in the concomitant lack of expectation of nurturing from others; for the more "demanding" patient one must remember that the same dynamics of hopelessness and self-loathing lie like pus just below each surface request. Not that such understanding cancels out the therapist's occasional exhaustion and less-than-admirable mutterings – "Who needs this!" has been heard to slip from my lips on certain dark nights. Nevertheless, given the patient's suicidal ideation and the evidence for the possibility of acting out, it is imperative for the therapist who takes cases such as those of Helen, Elaine, or Rose to be willing and able to be "on call," unless one wishes to proceed with supervised housing of the patient, as did the courageous Sechehaye (1951a,b) and Laing (Barnes and Berke, 1971). It would be ideal to have a foster-family home available as a short-term nurturant setting. However, the availability of such a situation is unlikely. In lieu of that, one could hospitalize the patient. Such protection is, of course, an option. However, the possible damage to the real-life functioning caused by such a choice would need to be weighed carefully against the risk of an actual suicidal attempt.

What can be done, then, given the patient's real needs and the therapist's human limitations? The best solution seems to be the awareness of the risks by both patient and therapist, and the therapist's commitment to only one such developmentally needy patient at any one time. I would also caution against doing such work with people who live without reliable adult support in their home—spouse, relative, or close friend. For the therapist's sanity, specifying available hours for calling can minimize inconvenience and interruption of personal time; the hours can be arranged according to the situation. Use of an office toy or a personal gift can function as a transitional object as it does for a child—sometimes for comfort, as a "sedative" representing the mother's breast (Winnicott, 1958i, pp. 235–236), sometimes as an object on which to project one's feelings. I have also found that a brief contact just before or after the workday will suffice to reduce the level of the patient's anxiety; the patient can come by to be assured of the therapist's existence and be sustained until the next official session.

It cannot be stressed strongly enough that the therapist should never accept such a case without receiving gratification from doing so. As in parenthood, the most successful hypno-play therapist is the one who enjoys a mutuality of pleasure with the child, who can form a Winnicottian "nursing couple" with that child. As Benedek wisely notes, not only the child is growing—there are "reciprocal ego developments" for the mother [parent] as that parent achieves "a new integration in her personality." But, again as in parenthood, the balance of needs and responsibilities is not equal: There is a big guy and a little guy. As Benedek (1959, p. 390) reminds us, "The infant's need for the mother is absolute, while the mother's for the infant is relative." The good-enough mother is she (or he!) who, at first, "keeps the world of the infant as simple as possible" (Winnicott, 1958j, p.245). Later, the mother adapts gradually to the infant's capacity to tolerate frustration and undertakes her "main task," that of the "disillusionment" of weaning (Winnicott, 1958j, p. 240).

Difficulties making the transition
from hypnotic to conscious work

Sometimes the patient has difficulty making the transition out of the play-therapy phase into the more conscious psychotherapeutic work. First of all, it is difficult for the patient to grow up, more difficult than it is for the normal child. Movement from one stage to the next involves loss, of course; but for children this loss is accompanied by physical maturation and the gains that result. The baby who trades in the softness of mother's lap for the hard floor is compensated by the thrill of learning to crawl; the baby who gives up the bottle is learning to drink from a cup and to eat new and interesting foods with a spoon. The adult patient, however, already knows how to walk and is familiar with those new taste sensations – all the adult patient feels, leaving, let us say, the lap, is the loss of the lap! And that lap is more important to the once-deprived adult than to the child who always had as much of it as was needed. Thus, transitions in which loss is involved must be handled with the awareness of the grief and with sensitivity to it. Better to hold on too long than to push faster; better to reach the point, usually no more than a few weeks later than the therapist would have chosen, where the patient becomes restive and pushes off into triumphant autonomy.

Even more important: Because of the idealized positive transference generated by the work in hypnosis in general, and regressive work in particular, the patient, functioning as an adult, may find it literally unthinkable to be angry or to express any negative feelings towards the therapist. There-fore, a problem that might not have arisen in more standard psychotherapy methods is created or exacerbated by the use of hypno-play therapy.

HELEN: WHEN FANTASIES EVAPORATE

Helen (see pp. 161–162) developed severe panic attacks and almost delusional hypochondriachal obsessions during later work in the years following the conclusion of play thera-py. It eventually became clear that just as her fantasies about her father and his ability to be the "safe" parent eva-porated, so did her fantasies about the therapist as the one who could be counted on to know everything, and to be infi-nitely "there" when called on. The containment of her rage over my imperfections and my other professional and per-sonal involvements expressed itself in obsessive concern for her own bodily survival.

This situation was very serious. The patient became al-most incapacitated and briefly psychotic in her delusional terror that "they" were destroying her through her bodily complaints (which had some physiological basis but were exacerbated by the intense anxiety). During the working-through of that phase, the patient complained, and I con-curred, that extended regressive work on an infant level might be expected to result in the experience of the destruc-tion of the patient's equilibrium when faith in the fantasy of the perfectly-safe-one dissolved.

Helen's case also makes it clear that the length of time during which the therapist needs to limit the number of other characterologically-damaged hypno-play therapy pa-tients may extend beyond the actual practice of age-regres-sive work. There must always be leeway for reinstituting extra hours for such patients as Helen. The importance of extending the period of time in which more than one day per week of therapy is available is therefore stressed, especially in situations where there is minimal family support. In this case it was almost a year before Helen was first able to tolerate being present with an ill person without "catching" the delusion of illness within herself. As she put it, "I did not like it, but I did not make that leap that it was happening to me. . . . It stayed in [the other person], it didn't travel to me."

The words of Winnicott (1958h, p. 202) are especially cogent in regard to this situation. As he puts it, "It seems to me doubtful whether a human child as he develops is capable of tolerating the full extent of his own hate in a sentimental environment. He needs hate to hate." It is all too easy to create such a "sentimental environment," in which the countertransferential hatred is repressed and denied, therefore giving no space to the inevitable hatred of the child (patient) for the parent (therapist). I do not doubt that such an atmosphere had developed to some extent in Helen's case. We must remember that it is not for nothing that "Rock-A-Bye Baby" is so slyly vicious! Again, therapists *must* monitor their own feelings honestly and find expression for them in such a way that the patient is not damaged, but is aware of their existence and can feel enabled to experience accurately aimed and appropriately proportioned anger. Such anger, in its clarity, separates the antagonists and in doing so draws boundaries without which psychosis has free rein.

Difficulties making the transition from regressed state to adult functioning

The patient may have difficulty making the transition to adult functioning for the rest of the day. Frequently the patient reports a sense of shifting "in and out" of young feelings during the working day, fearing inappropriate behavior with colleagues. Those with children say that they feel "too young" to be parents and are overwhelmed by the responsibility. Still others find themselves shifting "levels" from one moment to the next, unable to count on staying in one mode reliably, reacting to the therapist on the one hand with the intense transference of the hypnotic relationship, and on the other, as another adult. Still other patients may find it difficult to reconstitute at the end of the hour. The therapist may rightly be concerned for the patient's safety.

HELEN: MANAGING TO BE A PARENT

As a mother of latancy-age children, Helen found that she was temporarily unable to give "quality" mothering while she was involved in being mothered on an infant level herself. She reported that she did everything necessary for the children, providing their meals, clothing, and general caretaking, but did not want to do anything extra for them. This is less a problem of hypno-play therapy than it is one of depth-oriented psychotherapy and regressive work in general. When the parent is feeling like a child, but must function as a parent, the experience with play therapy can be and is an advantage. Helen was encouraged to play with her children and actually found that she could relate better to them in that situation than before. When necessary, such patients can be encouraged to make sure of auxiliary child care when possible — spouse, babysitters, grandparents, etc. — all of whom can be told that their assistance will be required only temporarily.

ELAINE: OSCILLATING BETWEEN CHILD
AND ADULT IN DAILY LIFE

Elaine expressed the longing to be part of my family, feeling simultaneously envious of my children and increasingly aware of the pleasure of being a separate adult and communicating on that level about topics of adult interest. It was discomfiting to find herself suddenly plunged into "littleness," almost without warning, at the precipitant of a look, tone of voice, choice of word, or other apparently minor cue from me.

This difficulty can be seen as a sign of movement, and interpreted as such. The patient can usually tolerate such instability when assured that it is temporary, due to the bifurcated aspect of child and adult work, and that it harbingers the onset of maturity in which an amalgam of the two is achieved. It is particularly helpful to make what can be called *blended interpretations* (see pp. 78–79) in which a symbolic story can be told during the hypnotic state and elements of it repeated in the conscious state. This method results in heightened interpretive impact, so that, as one patient put it, the integration of "two pictures that sometimes move together" can occur. In the above example, within less than a month the patient had made a vocational decision that hastened her entry into the fully credentialed world of her specialty.

Patient with a history of psychosis

DICK: A SAFE CONTEXT

Dick, an elderly widower, was seen as a referral from another therapist. The patient had been unable to recall any of his childhood, other than vague generalities. The primary therapist hoped that age regression, with or without play therapy, would be helpful for him. Being untrained in hypnosis, the therapist inquired as to the possibility of sending his patient for regressive work to a hypnotherapist. He reported that the patient's history included occasional auditory hallucinations with some paranoia.

I saw Dick in the presence of his primary therapist. Given the history, regressive work was undertaken extremely slowly, using the screen technique (See Chapter 8) with the patient beginning the process at the very back of a movie theatre, progressing towards the screen at his own pace. The actual "work" lasted only 30 minutes and consisted of a moving revivification of a Christmas at age 11, in which the patient spent the day alone, playing with his one new toy. He was able to cry, express his loneliness, and be comforted by me and his therapist, both of us playing gently with him, using several toy cars and trucks. Three hours were set aside for this session, giving considerable space for discussion and recompensation. The primary therapist had driven the patient to the appointment, and so was able to be in charge of driving the patient home and evaluating his capacity to function for the rest of the day. When the patient comes alone and the lack of recompensation is a surprise, the patient can remain in the waiting room and be seen again as necessary before being allowed to depart. The patient should, of course, never leave unaccompanied unless fully functional.

Discomfort with physical closeness

The therapist and/or patient may feel uncomfortable with the physical closeness common in early regressive hypno-play therapy; or either or both may feel uncomfortable with the knowledge of the previous physical closeness once conscious adult-oriented work is resumed. As we have said earlier, the hypnotic relationship is intense, primitive, and stimulating, involving the most basic of feelings concerning infancy – both being an infant and caring for one. Due to the power issues, it has been suggested that the hypnotic state may also "stimulate an oedipal transference with fantasies of seduction or competition" (Mott, 1982, p. 243). Note that again the fantasy goes two ways.

In addition to the above problems heightened by the use of hypnotherapy, hypno-play therapy adds another complication. The small child requires touching from the adults in his life – non-erotic casual touching that occurs during play, as well as nurturant touching, such as a pat or a hug. But the "child" in hypno-play therapy is, in body size and development, an adult. From the therapist's orientation, a response to the "child" as an adult body can be uncomfortable to say the least. And for the patient, even more so. For the patient, adult needs and desires can theoretically break in suddenly during regressive work and regularly carry through to unconscious and conscious expression in adult-adult work. This problem can occur with same-sex or opposite-sex combinations, depending on the sexual orientation of each, whether overt or, more dangerously, latent and denied. Recall the case of Yvonne (see Chapter 5). What if the therapist had harbored latent, denied homosexual tendencies? A noxious retraumatization of the patient, once seduced by her teacher, would have resulted, with disastrous implications. Obvious difficulties would result from a heterosexual attraction to a patient, the worst of which we know as blatantly unethical behavior on the part of the therapist who becomes personally involved with the patient on a sexual level. Thus, it is of the utmost importance that the therapist work in other ways than with hypno-play therapy if there is the smallest sense of out-of-control sexual impulses that might be engaged by physical contact with the patient – of either sex.

LARRY: AVOIDANCE OF SEXUALITY

Larry, a school principal, invariably dressed in conservative, well-pressed suits and perfectly knotted ties, was seen in a combination of conscious psychodynamic psychotherapy and hypno-play therapy, which mostly centered around preadolescence. Play therapy included only casual physical contact, as in passing an item from one to the other while sitting on the floor playing with construction toys and board games.

Larry had an unsatisfying marriage. He was frequently attracted by female co-workers and, as a nice-looking man, had many opportunities to have sexual liaisons with them. He resisted such invitations by "turning off" his sexual feelings, staying very busy with his work. Similarly, he evaded any sexualized material in the sessions, and the presence of that issue in the room, unmentioned and unmentionable, therefore became the only topic. Shortly following the recognition of this state of events, I pursued the matter in the conscious adult mode. In the next session Larry promptly reported a dream in which a female comes to sit next to him on the sofa, but as she sits down a white (doctor's) coat materializes over her clothing. An analysis of the dream led to the possibility of making explicit what had been covert, with resulting reduction in work-inhibiting tension.

The therapist must be aware of cues of his or her own discomfort, using those feelings as a barometer of the issue to be handled. It might be wise to go slowly, employing the medium of the stuffed animal with which to touch the patient, as was done for other reasons with Stan (See Chapter 6, p. 79). One must always be aware that, no matter how minimal physical contact may be, the regressive situation itself will intensify its effects through the actualized transference. It may be especially useful to make use of supervision or consultation around such situations. Most important, as stressed in the case above, is for the therapist to pay conscious attention to the problem and make it explicit before the covert aspect of it gains power.

ED: PROTECTION FROM OUT-OF-BOUNDS FEELINGS

Ed, a physician of casual dress and seemingly relaxed demeanor, sought therapy around his inability to commit himself to his work and become a successful practitioner. He was also troubled and frustrated in a neurotic long-term relationship with a woman whose sexual issues had led her to become unwilling to have intercourse with him. His history included a family in which sexual and other boundaries were fluid and in which sexual attraction among some of the family members bordered on the overt. Thus, any physical contact, such as a maternal touch on the shoulder or hand, was experienced by him as eroticized. During one phase of his hypnotic regressions, which did not include play therapy, he would often have highly sexualized fantasies, some symbolic and some directly concerning the therapist. The sexual content was so blatantly personalized, that in the conscious state the patient, although as a physician comfortable with the generalized aspect of discussion of the body, was embarrassed. Aware of the tightrope between warmth and eroticism with an attractive man, and simultaneously cognizant of the ways in which the patient needed to experience and introject a safe maternal presence, I also found the situation difficult to balance.

The therapist must be able to accept all of the patient's productions – otherwise there is no psychotherapy. At the same time, the therapist must be aware of the oedipal issues that have remained unresolved in the patient's unconscious, leading him or her to fantasize the seduction of or by the therapist (see Fromm, 1968, p. 79). The therapist's responsibility is to make sure that the patient feels protected from out-of-bounds feelings, and from the feelings of the therapist as well.

Therefore, in this situation, I chose to address the subject directly, in the conscious mode. I assured the patient that I respected his allowing himself to freely feel and associate, that his feelings were powerful expressions of his capacity to love, and that his love for me was an amalgam of his total life experience with those he had loved, from his parents, his siblings, his friends, and his lovers – his wishes and yearnings all merging seamlessly with his real-life adult contact with me. I told him that there would be a woman for him to love and to love him in the way that he wanted, a woman who would have a full relationship with him in his life. I told him that he could count on me to be his therapist and to care about him from that place.

It was not long after that session that the patient dissolved his unsatisfying affair and then met and became engaged to a colleague with whom he developed a deeply committed and passionate relationship, concluding in marriage. Simultaneously, his career stabilized in his finding satisfying work in a specialty in which he excelled. At a post-termination interview a year after the conclusion of therapy he shared a journal he had kept during the year, in which he wrote of finally saying goodby to his "nurturing, hypnotic mother," of "letting go of the cord," and a growing sense of missing "the collegial element of the therapeutic relationship."

Complexity of interpretation
at multiple levels

Since interpretation can be made on any or all developmental levels, the therapist has an especially complex task. The patient is, in fact, an adult, so interpretation on that level is likely appropriate when working in a psychodynamic mode. But the patient is also a child, perhaps children of various ages. Should separate interpretations be offered, depending on the stage at which the patient is functioning? Is interpretation appropriate at infant ages?

ELEANOR: A METAPHORICAL MESSAGE

Eleanor's mother had died suddenly when Eleanor was two. Grief was never addressed: Father remarried quickly, a new baby appeared. The empty feeling had pervaded Eleanor's life from that moment on. Doubtless there was anger ("She said she would come back"), perhaps guilt in Eleanor's construction of the loss. During age regression, Eleanor reexperienced the day in which her mother was carried off to the ambulance. At the moment, during this first excursion into the scene, only the tears and feelings of helplessness ("I can't change anything") filled the air.

Interpolated in the exit from trance I told a story about the lawn that she would see out the window when she opened her eyes: Due to an accidental oil spill from the lawnmower, one section of grass had died, leaving a bald place in which I had planted new seeds. I described my discouragement when, despite rain and sun, no new growth was visible. Somehow, I decided to wait just a bit longer—a little more time, a little more sun, and, at last, the grass, being of good quality seed, began to emerge. And now, from a distance, the grass appeared to be as one. Looked at more closely, however, one could see the bright-green, new-grass quality of the color, and one could, in fact, still make out the demarcation of the new and old.

Upon returning to the conscious mode, Eleanor looked

out on the grass. "I liked your story," she said. The relation-ship between the oil spill and the death, the tears and the rain, the sun and the love, the process of growth and develop-ment from the seeds of health did not need further interpre-tation at that time. The place for anger, guilt, and other defended affects had been set. I left the conscious-mode in-terpretation to just one sentence: "It is hard to return to the place of such emptiness, which must have seemed all the more empty given the fullness that had come before."

HELEN: PREVERBAL COMMUNICATION

A patient such as Helen (see above), for whom bottle feeding is part of the treatment, is obviously too "young" at that point to benefit from classical interpretation. That does not mean that the therapist does not talk to the patient. After all, the mother is not silent with her baby. Indeed, it seems to be built into the caretaker to talk to the object of that caretaking; even the fish breeder talks to the fish, and the plant lover to the plant. These "conversations" with the preverbal patient are a vital part of the corrective emotional experience, which is the mode in which, almost exclusively, one is working with such early regression. Speech with the "infant" is, from a literal view, one way; however, it is more dialogue than it seems. Like the loving parent, the therapist (parent) makes comments of general ego-supportive approv-al: "You are such a lovely little girl!" If the therapist is affec-tively engaged, these comments are accurate and true. In addition, the therapist supports behavior that may have been disapproved in the patient's infancy: "What a nice loud cry you can make when you want something." And attention is paid to labeling feelings and testing out the accuracy of that labeling: "Are you feeling hungry? Here (putting bottle in patient's mouth), is that what you want? (Patient begins to suck) You *are* hungry!"

In the parts of the sessions in which the patient is less regressed or functioning in the adult mode, whatever themes have been addressed in the early regression are continued.

Discussions and interpretations about other "hunger," about
the expression of needs and disowned feelings, link up without direct reference to the work in the hypno-play therapy
mode.

Among play therapists there are conflicting views about
the function and use of interpretation, especially when working with preschool children. The Kleinians will interpret
"down to the smallest detail" all play behavior, as if it were
the equivalent of the adult's free association or dreams, believing that "in its play the child acts instead of
speaking. . . ." (Klein, 1975, pp. 8–9). The Anna Freudians,
on the other hand, are more likely to use the play behavior of
the child to inform their own further structure of the analytic work. And more eclectic writers, such as Terr (1983, pp.
314–316), believe that interpretation is not necessary when
working with traumatic material that occurred between the
ages of two and four (with the implication that play therapy
is not done before the age of two), and that abreaction,
teamed with "corrective denouement," is sufficient for relief.

In hypno-play therapy, however, we have at least two, and
often more, ages of development to consider. Most economi-
cal in this situation is the blended interpretation, the story
that links the bifurcated experience of child and adult, helping to meld the two. There is, actually, nothing startling
about this idea: Many a "children's book," such as *Alice in
Wonderland*, is based on that premise, namely, that the story can be heard on multiple levels, remembered on one level
and reinterpreted from many other levels later.

EXTERNAL PROBLEMS

By *external problems* I refer to problems of professional
technique and environmental management. Although these
seem minor by comparison to the internal problems, if not
properly handled they can inhibit therapists from proceed-
ing. Therapists, in their dedication to helping their patients,
want to do the best possible – but they sometimes forget

that the word "possible" is part of the sentence and changes according to the total situation, including one's own level of experience. The "what if" sense of perfectionism is laudable, to some degree, of course, because it implies concern for doing the job right, for intolerance of sloppiness and inadequate preparation. But one cannot become experienced without first having been inexperienced! I hope there is no reader who expects to reach perfection; as I have not attained such a state of grace, I am ill-qualified to prepare others for that consummate achievement! This section will, however, address some of the more common problems inherent to hypno-play therapy. Why not take care of those we can take care of, since there will be so many none of us can forecast!

The resistant patient

Sometimes patients are resistant to the induction, to deepening, or to a particular segment of the hypnotic work. Here I am not referring to the common anxiety of naive subjects about the forthcoming experience of hypnosis, about which they have misconceptions based on popular beliefs. Education, including a demonstration through a prepared video, usually overcomes such anxiety, especially when a trusting relationship between patient and therapist already exists. I am speaking of the resistance that emerges in an experienced subject, resistance that seems likely correlated with the material to be explored.

Here the patient breaks out of trance entirely or, as in the case example of Tom in Chapter 5, becomes less and less productive. One patient, looking at the issue of his rage towards his father during an age regression, saw himself at the top of a steeple in danger of falling to his death if he didn't find a safe way to get down. Understandably, he could go no further in trance that day. The therapist must respect such resistance as important, as a positive sign of the patient's ability to monitor the pace of discovery and change. Madeleine, for example (see Chapter 9), would spring to her feet while in the midst of revivification of traumatic sexual expe-

riences. After pacing around the office for perhaps five minutes, during which she would repeat the material and estab-
lish it in her conscious mind, she would return to the couch
and, without further induction, return to trance state. For
other people, many weeks of conscious work may be required
before further exploration can be undertaken. In all cases,
the self-regulatory system of the patient determines the
pace of hypnotherapy.

A subset of the resistance problem needs particular men-
tion: the patient whose eyes open during or after a revivification or play therapy module, coming seemingly alert before
the exit procedure has been effected. When the material exposed has been traumatic, the therapist needs to make every
effort to reinduce trance, so as to provide the protective insu-
lation the situation most often demands (see Chapter 8).
Usually, reinduction is easily achieved, since the patient has
some residual trance sensations and is naturally motivated
to feel more comfortable. In the unlikely case in which the
patient does not reenter trance state, the therapist must
attend to the omission of a formal (although, perhaps unstructured) exit as an important and potentially problematic
state of events. The possibility of having inadvertently re-
traumatized the patient should be considered, and appropriate steps, such as extra telephone contact and perhaps an
additional session later in the day, should be taken.

More common is the kind of resistance exemplified in the
case example of Miriam (Chapter 4). Here the patient verbal-
izes her ambivalence ("Part of me wants to bolt and run, to
say I can't do it"); when her unconscious is given the option
of going on or coming awake, she yawns – a signal of deepening that has been established in earlier sessions – and continues, doing what becomes significant work. Hence the working rule is: When the signal is of a clear NO, the therapist
honors that decision, and returns to conscious work. When
the signal is a MAYBE, or an oscillating YES and NO, the
therapist provides the clear option for either and accepts the
result.

Last, of course, is the situation in which the patient, usually able to attain trance state easily, shows particularly peculiar resistance to doing so or to doing work in trance on a particular occasion. "Resistant" patients must be respected for their need to avoid particular work or particular depth of work. Picture the therapist who has worked diligently and creatively – and unsuccessfully – to induce trance in the patient. Or, more frequently, as in the case of Tom (see Chapter 5) trance has been achieved but the material dries up when the hypnotic state emerges. What is needed in such situations is the therapist's flexibility to allow for the possibility that a state of trance may not be useful! A permissive induction, such as one which asks the patient's unconscious to allow his or her eyes to close only "if this is the right time and place, and if trance will be useful for you now" is suitable in such situations. The following case example illustrates such a circumstance.

ANN: THE FUNCTION OF A "PERMISSIVE" INDIRECTION

Ann, generally an excellent subject with whom hypno-play therapy had been especially effective, was preparing to terminate. I had been somewhat insistent on her setting an exact date, given that decision. In the session in question, Ann brought in a terrifying dream in which she was shot to death in a ladies room by an unidentified man dressed like a "mobster," wearing a hat "with a band on it." On my suggestion, Ann rapidly went into trance, with the goal of understanding the meaning of the dream. Nothing happened – no image, no words – nothing. I finally inquired if Ann's unconscious felt that this was a matter to be best raised in consciousness. A prearranged ideomotor finger signal indicated "yes."

Returning to the conscious state, Ann worked on the dream, which pointed towards her repressed feeling of anger at me for having pushed her to set a specific termination date. She identified the man as my "male" intellectual side, opposing her female, feeling side. My maleness, taking theory rather than feeling as its guide, was "terminating" (killing) her like a cold-blooded hit man. She further interpreted the description of the hat by identifying the pun of "a band on" with "abandon" – I was abandoning her.

On her way to the conclusion of her work with me, Ann needed to confront me with her anger as one adult to another, not as regressed patient to therapist. Unconsciously oriented hypnotherapy was not appropriate in this case, and it did not work.

The mute or preverbal patient

What happens when the patient does not talk in trance, either in general or under certain circumstances, such as during regression to preverbal ages or to traumatic events? As has been mentioned in Chapter 8, the patient who is silent in trance is not rare. Speaking is an effort in trance and often feels disruptive to the patient. Unfortunately, this silence causes most therapists to feel somewhat helpless and perhaps fairly anxious. Let me stress that *there is nothing wrong with the patient's remaining silent.*

One fairly common cause of elective mutism is early trauma: The shock of the trauma may have triggered that reaction, or there may have been some explicit or perceived prohibition against talking about it (see the case of Charlotte, below). In such situations, other means of communication can be found through artistic, musical, or athletic activities, through the use of puppets, and through wordless role-play and pantomime.

For the preverbal "child," the situation is somewhat different. Being nonverbal is not a problem to that patient – it is only a problem to the therapist who finds it a problem! Perhaps seasoned parents will find this situation least disorienting; just being with the baby, finding one's body sensitive to that of the child, is all that is required at this most primitive stage of the patient's development. It is even possible for the patient to remain silent throughout the entire trance, making no sound at all, or babbling in preverbal syllables, or crying wordlessly. In such situations, the therapist speaks, just as a parent would automatically speak to a baby who cannot answer. The "parent" can play nonverbal games such as peek-a-boo, sing songs, recite nursery rhymes, offer a game of banging pots with a wooden spoon, and so forth. If the patient is distressed, the "parent" can hold the patient, give the patient a stuffed animal or blanket, feed the patient from a nursing bottle, talk to the patient to identify the feelings ("Are you feeling hungry?"), and express general sympathy ("That's too bad you're so sad right now") and interest ("I wish I knew why you're so angry") in simple language. At other times the patient's use of ideomotor signaling, such as the automatic raising of a finger, can be encouraged; similarly, conscious signaling, such as head-nodding, is commonly employed.

Silence may also be the result of what Kluft (1985) refers to as "autohypnotic withdrawal," commonly seen in childhood multiple personality disorders, and other situations in which the best defense proved to be total emotional escape. The same methods as would be used with the preverbal "child" are appropriate, as the therapist, by gentle caretaking, coaxes the patient out of the autistic adaptation that has served as protection against pain.

CHARLOTTE: INJUNCTIONS AGAINST "TELLING"

A fast-food cook in her early twenties, Charlotte was married to an immature unemployed man, really a boy several years younger than she. Although she was quite bright and adequate to the task of filling out complex clinic forms, she had not completed high school, never read for pleasure, and spoke with a stammer. She had become pregnant ostensibly to please her husband, as she felt she had nothing else to offer. Her eyes darted anxiously about the room as she described her distaste for any physical contact. She found sexual relations virtually intolerable.

At times during a session, perhaps due to affective overload, Charlotte would stare vacantly into thin air. She claimed amnesia for a good deal of her childhood. During an age regression she made sounds of distress but was unable to speak, and afterwards stated that she could not remember what had occurred. In subsequent days she had many violent, sexual dreams which she reported. She finally acknowledged that she could not "tell" what had happened, as she had been told that she would be killed if she "ever said a word." It was necessary to take that injunction literally, as would a small child, and to join the patient in agreeing that "telling" would not be necessary. Instead, sessions consisted of composing an "opera" using hand puppets in which the characters sang, rather than spoke, the story. What emerged was the memory of rape by Charlotte's father when she was four, which she had remembered and reexperienced during the silent regression. Subsequently the patient asked her sisters about their experiences and discovered that all of them had been abused in the same way.

HELEN: REGRESSION TO INFANCY

Helen, whom we have met before, was an extremely intelligent woman in her thirties. As an infant she had been neglected and "failed to thrive." Because of the lack of early maternal bonding and resultant nutritional insufficiency, for about nine months of therapy she spent each twice-weekly therapeutic session (two hours each) in trance state, during which she was fed with a nursing bottle. During that period, part of her was regressed to infancy; obviously, not all of her adult functions were suppressed, as she did not lose control of her bladder and bowel functions, as can be true with those whose adult adaptations are of lower functioning (see, for example, Barnes and Berke, 1971). Nevertheless, this patient did become nonverbal or, as I saw it, preverbal, responding very like an infant to simple, repetitive rhythmical language, nursery songs, rocking and other soothing behaviors. After about nine months, she became tired of the bottle, rejecting it over a few sessions' time, and moving on to behaviors more common to the toddler.

Furnishings

The therapist's office should not be furnished in such a way that play materials threaten its decor. If the therapist is going to worry about the survival of the objects in the office, the patient will never play freely. As in families where furnishings are highly prized, but children are at least equally regarded, solutions have been found that can transfer to many office situations. A play corner can be arranged so that the materials there either are not fragile or are expendable and replaceable. When making purchases, one's favorite label should read WASHABLE. Duplicates of play items should be easily obtainable. This is not the place for the exquisite English bone china teacup; even if the therapist doesn't care about its fate, the patient, both as child and as adult, will feel distressed if it breaks. A washable area rug over any general carpeting can minimize damage due to spills and stains; a plain tile surface in the area that is at risk, while less cozy, is even simpler.

Similarly, when choosing clothing, the therapist should consider the possibility of sitting or crawling on the floor. Since the hypno-play therapist, as therapist to adults, may dress more formally than many child play therapists do, painting smocks or other coveralls can provide a solution. A coverall for the patient will often also be appreciated.

Noise level

For those practitioners whose work is centered in a clinic or in a group practice with shared multi-office surroundings, noise can be a serious problem. On the one hand, quiet surroundings are usually most conducive, though not absolutely necessary, to induction. Yet the clinic setting often finds such an ideal climate marred by typing, by conversations outside one's door, by the racket made by the inevitable repair people, by honking horns, etc. On the other hand, play therapy is often noisy, and should be. The patient, and perhaps the therapist as well, may bang, yell, jump: Think of the behavior of young children on a playground, and then translate the same behavior into adult bodies. Still, one's colleagues do deserve consideration!

There seems to be no perfect solution to this problem, only a host of compromises, with which most child therapists have grappled. Sound-proofing is an expensive option. In its stead one can try to schedule hypno-play therapy sessions during one's neighbors' lunch hours; white-noise machines placed outside the door can mask some of the lower decibel noise; carpeting on the floor and blankets hung on doors and inside walls can reduce some of the carry-power of the sound. Let us hope that our colleagues will be understanding. It is even possible that a colleague may be interested in observing, with the patient's permission, this interesting method of treatment.

Scheduling

The patient, being deeply regressed, may need more than an hour session in order to reconstitute and to integrate the experience into an adult mode. Consequently, in choosing to work in hypno-play therapy one should plan the schedule to allow for long sessions, preferably with some latitude for extension, and with the possibility for an extra visit at day's end. As discussed earlier (Chapter 9), patients remain in a slight trance state for several minutes after they think that trance has been terminated; hypnotherapists are routinely advised in training to treat the post-trance period as if the patient were still in trance, assuming the patient is susceptible to trance logic and choosing his or her words as if they will be taken literally. When in deep trance, especially after age regression, most patients find it particularly difficult to return to the full appreciation of the here and now. One patient, aware that she had to leave for work, appeared to be reconstituted after an hour of deep early work, but found herself puzzled upon looking at the office analog clock, trying to recall how to tell time! Obviously, if only in the interests of safety, the patient should not be leaving the office until fully capable of dealing with the realities of life, such as operating a motor vehicle or crossing a street. Ideally, it would be possible to arrange to have the patient sit in the waiting room until fully reconstituted or to have another person available as potential assistant or companion. However, when such arrangements are difficult, or when the situation arises without prior planning, the therapist must have some slack in the schedule to allow for the patient's possibly protracted recovery time.

If, as recommended, the number of long-term hypno-play therapy patients is strictly limited, this organization should be within the realm of possibility. One can, for example, schedule such patients for, say, the period before lunch or dinner or as the last session of the day. As mentioned, sessions of one-and-a-half or two hours are most frequently ideal for the comfort of the patient, whose ego is being buffeted from one stage to the other in a most disquieting manner.

AFTERWORD ON THE TOPIC OF TRAINING

This chapter has addressed some problems of significant concern to practitioners of hypno-play therapy. I have assumed the reader's basic knowledge of the use of hypnosis, in which excellent training, as provided by the American Society of Clinical Hypnosis and the Society for Clinical and Experimental Hypnosis, is readily available. But the biggest problem is that of having or anticipating problems with nowhere to take them. The responsible therapist hesitates to venture into the unknown, especially when no formalized program of training or expert consultation is offered. And rightly so! Psychotherapy of any sort is to be taken as nothing less than a professional commitment to the patient. In addition to pressing for the creation of such training in hypno-play therapy, I encourage the reader to use videotaping for self and peer supervision; to form supervision groups for support, mutual education and criticism; and to practice with colleagues, taking the roles of both patient and therapist, using the models presented in this book, and moving to specific cases from current cases of concern. Child therapists and specialists in developmental psychology can be useful consultants for the design of play components.

It would seem sensible, when beginning to use hypno-play therapy with patients, to work up from the simpler to the more complex cases. The prudent beginning driver, trained and tested at 35 miles per hour, does not accelerate to 55 when leaving the Registry! In lieu of further driving instruction, one inches up, first to 40, then 45, then 50, bit by bit, until 55 miles per hour feels natural.

11

THE CHOICE OF HYPNO-PLAY THERAPY

Is hypno-play therapy *the answer*? Certainly not. It is another technique whose benefits the eclectically-minded therapist trained in hypnotherapy can consider. There seems to be a certain inevitability to the Hegelian life-cycle for movements in all fields: a thesis-antithesis-synthesis pattern. So too for hypnosis. The swing is currently favorable, replacing the disrepute which shrouded this approach during the first half of this century. The value of hypnosis in curing *some* physical and mental diseases rapidly becomes a veritable credo that it is a wondrous method that can cure *all* physical and mental diseases. . . . and then, when that fails, that it can cure nothing. Let me enter a plea for the rejection of magical thinking and its replacement by rationality. Like psychotherapy, hypnosis in general, and age regression and hypno-play therapy in particular, are valuable when applied by *some* therapists with *some* patients for *some* issues at *some* times. One must consider the circumstances.

QUESTIONS TO CONSIDER

What is the issue at hand for the patient?

Just as play therapy is generally not the mode of choice for children over the age of 12 (Lebo, 1951, 1956), so play therapy with children's toys is inappropriate for issues that

are squarely those of adolescence or beyond. A woman who
has been raped during adulthood does not need to act out
the rape with dolls and puppets – unless, in her history, there
are earlier associations with sexual abuse or other related
issues in childhood. Thus the rule of thumb can be developed
as follows: If the issue stems from adulthood, work can proceed with the therapist's customary techniques. As the history of the issue emerges, hypno-play therapy may become a
peripheral adjunct, as in the case of Yvonne (see Chapter 5),
or more and more a central option.

What are the hazards of working in a regressive mode with the patient?

Here, intrapsychic diagnosis teamed with evaluation of
the patient's life circumstances is vital. Assuming an outpatient setting, the therapist must be assured that the patient
is capable of recompensating sufficiently to proceed with life
to at least a moderate extent, unless there is in-home caretaking by a professional person. In the rare circumstance
where extensive nursing care is necessary, it is best to have a
paid person rather than a family member, to minimize a shift
of the family system in which the patient will be put in the
role of the "sick" member and kept there by the now-altered
system long after such protectiveness is necessary. The patient must have people who care, who can be telephoned,
who will give the support when needed, and who will return
to a more balanced relationship as soon as appropriate. Until
such time, as a support network is in place, age regression is
probably unadvisable. For the schizoid or apathetically depressed person who may have no such relationships, regressive work must go slowly enough that such relationships can
begin to build and become workable along with the therapeutic process; in such situations, the therapist serves temporarily as the transitional object between the patient and
the rest of the world.

The issue of diagnosis is not being ignored. It is true that
I have applied diagnostic terminology sparingly, and have

made only passing reference to formal *DSM-III* diagnoses in a few of the case studies and examples in this book. The omission of diagnoses does not arise from my opposition to using them. In fact, it is almost always valuable to actively consider the ramifications of the particular constellations of history and symptom manifestations in terms of the current conventional labels of the mental health professions. A humanistic stance need find no contradiction in the consideration of the patient as a person rather than as a disease, and in the use of specialized terminology to describe some aspects of that person's physical and emotional being. Diagnostic labels, used descriptively rather than punitively, can greatly enhance the therapist's ability, when applied in order to expand a limited-angle lens rather than to close it further. One can communicate with one's colleagues, as well as read and learn more productively, when one owns the vocabulary by which to locate and share possibly relevant information.

Why, then, have I mostly eschewed the assignment of diagnostic labels in the cases discussed? Among the myths surrounding hypnotherapy are the beliefs that certain types of personalities are unhypnotizable and that others present such hazards that only the foolhardy would employ hypnosis with them. We are warned repeatedly of the "*danger of precipitating a psychiatric illness*," of "*making [the] existing disorder worse*," especially with schizophrenic or suicidal patients (West and Deckert, 1965, pp. 95–96, italics theirs), of producing "untoward results," especially psychosis precipitated by that technique (Auerbach, 1962). The January 1987 issue of the *American Journal of Clinical Hypnosis* features five articles dealing with adverse effects of hypnosis, most of them caused by experiences with untrained, lay, or inappropriately trained practitioners (such as dentists operating outside their specialty). Although the editor concludes that "hypnosis, when properly used, is one of the safest tools in the healing professions," he properly advises that "we need to be more aware of the possible adverse effects when it is misused" (Mott, 1987, 148).

Similarly, Judd, Barrows and Dennerstein (1986, p. 59), in

an article investigating the same topic, find that "age regression was the activity in hypnosis most often associated with
reported negative sequelae," and that "adverse effects appear
to be associated with lack of knowledge and experience, poor
patient assessment, poor therapeutic technique and with
specific aspects of the patient-therapist relationship, rather
than hypnosis per se". Responsible therapists will take these
warnings to heart. However, it was my intention that the
reader be encouraged to think freely about a wide range of
patients for whom hypnotherapy with age regression, with
or without play, has been used successfully before attending
to the hazards that might be inherent in a particular situation.

As an interesting exercise, the reader could act as potential therapist to some of the patients whose cases have been
presented earlier in this book. To that end, the next section
will offer a synopsis of some of these cases. Reading each
through, as if seeing each for the first time, the reader might
begin by attempting a tentative *DSM-III* diagnosis such as
is usual after one or two sessions of initial evaluation. Then
the reader might ask, "Given that diagnosis, would I recommend the use of age regression or hypno-play therapy as a
treatment? How could such treatment advance the course of
therapy? Would such treatment be dangerous?"

Having addressed the intellectual aspects of such an evaluation, the reader will also attend to the particular and perhaps countertransferential emotional reactions to the decision to treat or not to treat the patient using regressive
work: "Am I feeling anxious about using hypnosis and/or
hypno-play therapy with this patient? Am I feeling curious?
Excited? What are my feelings and, given my personal history, what are they telling me about the patient? About my
readiness to proceed with a new modality?" Observing each
reaction in turn gives the therapist the opportunity to notice
the specific issues that surround particular syndromes or
histories. All of these data will help the therapist prepare for
the real-life decisions that will all too soon have to be made.

CASE HISTORIES IN SYNOPSIS

Helen: An attractive, middle-aged mother, she was the oldest in a sibship of two. As an infant she suffered from nutritional deprivation, probably caused by a failure-to-thrive syndrome. Although of normal weight, she reported a struggle with food, hoarding and overeating when distressed. At first interview, presenting problems included marital difficulties and several phobias. She regularly experienced panic attacks surrounding everyday common leave-takings of children and husband. With a history of allergy to many medications, she was in excellent health. Nevertheless, she was hypochondriacal and occasionally delusional about bodily symptoms; some symptoms had their roots in physical fact, others no reality at all. She described herself as having been a frightened child whose facial expression was one of continuous pouting. One incident she particularly recalled was of thinking that the adults had changed the clocks to torture her, as she had not been aware that several hours had passed since lunchtime. Of high intelligence, she was a college dropout with a poor academic record. She had several good relationships with male and female friends.

Elaine: A middle-aged lawyer, married, with three children, she came with the complaint of feelings of worthlessness despite her obvious brilliance and many outstanding artistic and athletic skills. She was unable to achieve advancement in her specialty because of her lack of belief in her capacities, and the resulting lack of concrete achievements necessary. When under stress she often practiced self-mutilation. She was given to emotional outbursts of crying, yelling, and physical behavior resembling the tantrums of a two-year-old; during fights with her husband they sometimes hit each other. She obsessed almost daily about suicide and had made one serious attempt in the past. She stated that she would never "try" suicide again – that if she decided to commit suicide, she would succeed. Her fantasies and dreams included violent, gory material juxtaposed with images of emptiness and terror. She did not share the more frightening feelings with her family or friends, although she had several close relationships with males and females.

Dick: An elderly single accountant, Dick had been hospitalized in his middle years for depression which included psychotic symptoms such as auditory hallucinations. He reported sexual obsessions surrounding a four-year-old neighborhood child, although he had not acted on them. He had a paranoid attitude towards life, although the paranoia did not reach psychotic proportions. He seemed to have no friends, and worked in an isolated situation. He recalled almost nothing of his childhood.

Charlotte: This young fast-food cook, married to an immature unemployed man several years her junior, had a history including rape by her father at the age of four. She spoke with a stammer. She had been hospitalized about five times after suicide attempts, and had been given a course of ECT one of those times. She often related in a totally depersonalized manner, looking blankly ahead of her for several minutes at a time, as if in a petit mal seizure (for which tests proved negative), whenever her anxiety level rose too high. She often abused alcohol and prescription drugs, especially tranquilizers.

Barbara, a middle-aged divorced woman in her forties, was of high intelligence but functioned in low-level, isolated jobs due to chronic depression. A pleasant, soft-spoken person, she had only one or two close friends and felt too uncomfortable to attend social events such as parties. She had attempted suicide during her twenties and had been in therapy with several different therapists since that time. A parentified child, she was caretaker to her younger siblings, all of whom had also attempted suicide during adulthood. A single parent, she was uncertain whether her sexual preference was for men or for women.

Yvonne, a graduate student in architecture, considered herself a lesbian. Her presenting problem was extreme distress including anxiety and depression around the terminal illness of the older woman, once her teacher, who had been her first homosexual partner. She had a stormy (platonic) relationship with one female friend, and a few other nonsexual intense relationships with males and females.

Madeleine: A painter in her twenties, Madeleine came around her suspicion that her sexual inhibitions were related to some act or acts of incest that she could not remember. Her history included many moves of residence from country to country in Europe, during her childhood, due to her father's work. As a teenager she was involved in several sexual relationships with older men; although she did not participate in the perpetration of crimes, she associated with people on the fringes of the criminal community, leading her to become involved in situations in which she was raped and exposed to other physical and legal jeopardy. During this era she also went through periods of drug abuse and bulimia, both of which had abated. Her life at the time of intake was somewhat Bohemian, but health-oriented and far more "respectable" than it had been ten years earlier. She had several female friends, cohabited in a long-term monogamous heterosexual relationship, and associated with a community of other artists.

Nadine: Brutally treated by her mother as a child, unprotected by her alcoholic father, Nadine had superficially made an excellent adjustment to life. Attractive and well-spoken, the mother of two children, she had been married a short time to her second husband, a widower with his own children. She was employed regularly, and enjoyed many good friends. Having once been in therapy for several years, she felt that many of her issues had been resolved. Her presenting problem was agoraphobia and acrophobia, which were crescendoing to a degree of serious incapacitation.

Otto: Severely depressed, Otto could hardly walk into the office. Almost mute, he responded to questions with one word answers or head nods only. Both Otto's grandfather and father, construction workers, had been killed in job-related accidents; now Otto practiced the same occupation. Otto's father had died when Otto was eight years old; Otto's oldest child was seven, the youngest two. Otto seemed to have a few friends with whom he played a variety of sports.

Victor: This 25-year-old programmer came to treatment around his concerns about what he feared was an addiction to gambling that was ruining his marriage. He also reported that his wife complained about his lack of "patience," which led him to have near-violent arguments with her as well as with others, including his boss. Of good intelligence, Victor showed no insight into his behavior and related most events with total lack of all affect except anger. He described vivid fantasies of murder and mutilation regarding those he felt had wronged him by calling him derogatory names, by winning at poker "unfairly," and so forth. Although he had not attempted retribution, he did smash holes in walls and break furniture when angry. He seemed to have no close friends, but maintained a relationship with a few of his many siblings.

Bill: A Black administrator in an all-white bank, this middle-aged married man suffered from high blood pressure and hyperhydrosis. He came requesting treatment for stress. His issues surrounded his position as a Black in a white world. He was ever vigilant, ever one step ahead of the game, ever subliminally anxious.

Most likely the reader has noted some hallmark characteristics of the borderline personality, aspects of the narcissistic character disorders, and some psychosis along with the (neurotic) dysfunctions or more relatively benign adjustment disorders. Given a conventionally structured written diagnostic evaluation of these people, by, let us say, a referring practitioner, the intelligent and conservative psychotherapist might well have eliminated many of them from consideration for regressive hypnosis. At the least, although perhaps experienced with people of the same general description, the therapist might have an additional sense of wariness, a feeling of insecurity in handling such work.

There is nothing wrong with caution—but there is something wrong with caution that prevents efforts that can facilitate the movement the patient needs. When in doubt, it is in everyone's best interests for the therapist to consult with experienced colleagues, whether involved in the case or not, who might even sit in and observe or assist, having previously discussed that possibility with the patient. In some clinic settings, having a consultant or team behind the one-way mirror is an excellent means of getting support and supervision. Many creative solutions lie in the wings. If the concern is for the patient's capacity to reconstitute, for example, one can call upon the services of a student to accompany the patient on a walk or sit with the patient for a while in another office or waiting room after the session. The lesson is this: Rather than eliminate the possibility of regressive work with the more seriously disturbed patient, consider other creative approaches to expand the safety net as needed—whether by patient or by therapist.

Who might be at risk?

The currently psychotic patient may, in fact, respond very well to hypnosis, as has been amply demonstrated in the literature (see, for example, Scagnelli-Jobsis, 1982). Given the theoretical stance that non-organic psychotic symptoms represent early developmental failures, the hypno-play therapy orientation seems innately sensible. However, the first order of business in working with a flagrantly psychotic patient is usually to resurrect rather than to blur the boundaries between present and past, conscious and unconscious, so as to hasten the patient's reentry into the world of here and now. The increase in dependency that usually occurs with the extensive use of age regression needs to be managed carefully, so as to increase the positive transference, which can facilitate such reentry without fostering the patient's sense of helplessness. Carefully applied, hypnosis can, as Sands (1986, p. 229) notes, provide a place "which is neither too close and controlling nor so distant as to be felt as abandoning, and which serves as the basis for a transference and its exploration." After a psychotic break hypnosis can be used to further reconstitution. One manic-depressive woman described her experience with hypno-play therapy as one that helped her "mend the division" of her being.

The hypnotherapist must always be careful not to "suggest" symptom removal when the symptom has served as a defense to further decompensation; as West and Deckert (1965) and many others point out, such treatment could be harmful in the extreme, leading to further disintegration, including possible suicide. Indeed, in the aforementioned article by Auerbach (1962), removal of symptoms or habits, such as pain, overeating, and smoking was reported to be a common cause of the iatrogenic psychosis. Rather, if hypnosis is to be used at all, methods of symptom substitution rather than removal are recommended, with the stress on the present rather than on the past serving the goal of more adaptive in-the-world functioning.

However, as always, there are exceptions to the above statements, especially where the psychosis is limited to psychotic lacunae rather than pervasive. For example, hypnotic regression has been used successfully in work with multiple personalities, leading towards the fusion of the personalities into an integrated whole (see, for example, Kluft, 1982). The use of hypno-play therapy in such cases could hasten that process in working with the personalities whose ages are appropriate for such an approach. I can also see particular applicability of regressive hypnotic work for hysterical conversion symptoms, which are in themselves delusional and hence in the psychotic category. When the etiology of these symptoms is lost in an amnesic cover, the use of age regression, again with or without play therapy as relevant to the emerging material, can facilitate recovery. In both of these categories, regressive work, which can include play therapy when called for, helps to resolve by positive means damage otherwise expressed through psychotic representations of reality.

The actively suicidal, violent, or otherwise dangerous person is always a high-risk patient. Working in regressive hypnosis may activate uncontrollable behaviors. Such work is best undertaken in the structure of inpatient settings where staff are knowledgeable and cooperate with the goals and efforts of the primary therapist. Formerly suicidal patients, including those considered borderline, can often benefit greatly from hypno-play therapy, especially after significant progress has been made in establishing reliable trust with the therapist. A hospital environment will usually not be required. Experiences with the reliable "good" mother can literally be vital in establishing an antidote to the horrendous, empty depressive despair, isolation, rage, and terror that envelop many such patients.

The patient who is severely afraid of losing control might or might not benefit from age regression with or without hypno-play therapy. Let us stipulate that this person has established the necessary trusting relationship with the therapist and has been given the chance to understand the process and purpose of the procedure being considered; nevertheless, terror predominates. I do not assume that I am dealing with a latent psychosis, although that possibility must be kept in mind. My experience does not confirm the findings of Brown and Beletsis (1986, pp. 100–101), who note, for example, that children of alcoholics, for whom "being a child carried nothing but fear and feelings of helplessness," experience the "promise of regression . . . as a terrifying loss of control." That was not so for Nadine, for example (see Chapter 7). In addition, many patients whose parents were not alcoholic fit into that description of childhood. Fear of loss of control can be paralyzing; this fear is best respected. In such instances, age regression should be eschewed for the time being. It is a violation of empathy to try to talk the patient into "trying" the experience by lecturing about the fact that hypnosis is, in some ways, an intensification of control. Instead, one can use the opportunity to investigate the issue of control. The therapist might, for example, suggest that the patient have a dream that might cast light on the terror that "losing control" brings up.

The patient suffering from post-traumatic stress syndrome may be inappropriate for direct regressive work. In particular, those suffering from what Brown and Fromm (1986) call "complicated" (rather than "simple") PTSD are at risk of "intrusive experiences" brought on by abreactive work; for them, especially, carefully "dosed" experiences of emotional expression are needed to prepare for the desired goal of integration. However, after careful evaluation, the patient who does not need to be excluded may greatly benefit from regressive work, with or without play therapy as indicated by the material that emerges. It should be noted that although the precipitating trauma may stem from adult occurrences, earlier events may have predisposed the patient to the amnesic response; these may be best treated with play therapy. What is more, even the patient who is excluded, as by Brown and Fromm's (1986) criteria, may eventually reach the phase of "facilitation of self-development which was arrested by the traumatization and the integration of the traumatic events as an accepted fact of . . . life." In that stage of therapy, Brown and Fromm recommend a "playful therapeutic atmosphere" (p. 510). Hypno-play therapy is made to order.

The patient with certain serious medical problems should be carefully evaluated before being accepted for regressive work. Patients suffering from grand mal epilepsy could be at risk in doing hypnotic work, since regression may trigger memories of a major seizure, precipitating repetitions for which the therapist may not be prepared. And even if the therapist is prepared, the possible benefits of the age regression need to be weighed against the additional occurrence of seizure for the patient. Patients with severe asthma conditions should be watched carefully for oncoming attacks leading to severe respiratory distress; their medications should be on hand should an emergency arise. Patients who have serious heart conditions or are prone to stroke also should be evaluated carefully before embarking on age regression; the material that might emerge might be more than their damaged body can handle. Of course, these cautions are appropriate to all psychotherapy; the additional risk concerns the patient's experience of strong affect and the lessened strength of the defenses during trance.

Patients taking mood-altering drugs, including alcohol, at the time of proposed induction should be informed that hypnotherapy (like psychotherapy in general) is only practiced with patients whose conscious mind is fully available. Otherwise, to what will such patients reconstitute? The therapist can point out that hypnosis is not another "trip," but is serious work and needs to be done in that light.

Thus, with these few exceptions, most of which have exceptions themselves, regressive hypnosis with play therapy can be treated as an available and especially valuable option, when the circumstances make such work feasible and relevant.

12

THE BENEFITS OF
HYPNO-PLAY THERAPY

> I'm beginning to get a sense of who I am and the possi-
> bilities that come from knowing these places inside my-
> self, and having access to them, and at the same time
> learning to use them and have control over them.
>
> — Elaine, about a year after beginning
> hypno-play therapy

Surely every therapist has wished that many of the adults
in treatment had been taken for help when they were young.
If only the problem could have been addressed then, how
much simpler the solution would have been, how many years
of desperation or, at the least, restriction could have been
eliminated!

Yet, even child therapy has its built-in limitations, especially in the more serious cases: The child usually must return for most of the week to the very home in which the
issues have most often arisen. Family systems are complex,
often involving interrelated and enmeshed conflicts, compromises, neurotic adjustments, pathological behaviors. Family
therapy, frequently the treatment of choice, is usually resisted and frequently unworkable; for example, a careful
study by Kaplun and Reich (1976) "does not tend to support
the belief that severely abusing parents are receptive to
counseling or psychotherapy; the extreme, long-standing
psychopathology, the host of coexisting problems, and the

paucity of insight and motivation all tend to point against this view for most cases." In the majority of their case examples, the family simply didn't show up for their appointments. Where family therapy is, in fact, initiated, parents commonly resent the position of superiority of the therapist, the outsider to whom the child's attachment grows, the one whose very success only points out their deficits the more. The therapist must walk a very narrow line to avoid making the situation worse for the child at home.

Of course, the more that can be done sooner, the better. I rejoice and am in awe of the fine family and child work that triumphs over the odds. In fact, the use of hypno-play therapy with my adult parents has made them amenable, even enthusiastic, about supporting individual or family work with their own children when that has become advisable, for they have learned to identify with themselves as children, and hence have become capable of a new empathy with their own children.

As stated at the outset of this book, most practitioners of hypnotherapy follow Spiegel et al. (1981, p. 239) in the definition of hypnosis as "a method of disciplined concentration which can be used adjunctively with a primary treatment strategy." In general, that view is valid. Hypno-play therapy, however, is a treatment modality in and of itself. It is the best way I have encountered to meet the person at the place(s) at which the damage was done, to repair it, and to move through and past it. One hypno-play therapy patient began treatment reporting dreams of violent, vicious animals, and of houses with holes in the floors and walls. A year later she spoke of the existence of "a bottom" from which she recognized the emergence of an embryonic "sense of forgiveness." Obviously, I do not believe that early damage is irreversible. But, I am also not saying that all such damage *is* reversible. Reconstruction cannot produce the same results as a "good enough" early development. Perhaps most but not all of the holes will be filled, or perhaps the paint will not quite match that of the original, leaving an uneven coloration. The animals may be more or less tamed, or may recede into the nonthreatening distant landscape. This book presupposes the existence of age-related periods in which original learning is intended to occur. Nevertheless, human beings have an amazing degree of flexibility in their capacity to work through the damage and deficits of the past long after the original period at which development should have naturally appeared. Evidence of this "capacity for resilience" with both animals and humans is reviewed by Kagan (1980, p. 140ff); another more partisan volume in opposition to the "critical period" theory is that by Clarke and Clarke (1976).

I do not imply that the now healthy patient does not remember the original traumas, the years of pain, the losses. The difference is that the patient no longer *suffers* from them. Gone, or at least greatly reduced, are the restrictions on the being and on the expression of self. The physical and emotional symptoms, often the presenting problems, disappear or are mostly alleviated.

All those who have taught children have come to recognize that their learning is not linear. Rather, it proceeds with leaps both backward and forward, spirals, swirls, and undefinable patterns of movement to which the teacher must be ever adaptable. Life is not without sorrow, pain, and anxiety—but it also is not without joy, comfort, and tranquility. All or mostly all of the empty places can be filled, so that hunger is not the motivating force. There can finally be room for the energy of growth and creativity.

The classical analyst's "internal position" is always, at bottom, a struggle for "a new and better childhood" for the patient (Racker, 1968, p. 33). With that goal in mind, I have become a pragmatic psychotherapist as well as a theoretician, a reversal of priority from an earlier, more academic orientation. Hypno-play therapy works for many for whom traditional methods do not work at all or for whom many years are required in order to produce results satisfying to the patient: the character/personality disorders in particular fall into this category. To be able to reach down into the chasm and create the capacity for object relations is a remarkable experience. I cannot say honestly that I do this work only for the good of the patient; I too grow from my participation in the partnership.

If the reader can forgive a cliché, I think of each patient as a potential work of living art or music. The capacity for integrity of self is innate in every human being, but the environment sometimes forbids and punishes its appearance. At the least it often does not provide the permission and the tools for its development and expression. As a therapist, my work is to address that capacity, to provide the environment to nurture it, whatever *it* might turn out to be. Each time, with each individual, my personal and professional objective is to discover the individual's uniqueness, and my pleasure to eventually view and come to appreciate the particular work of art, to hear that particular, special song that results.

REFERENCES

Alexander, F. (1961). *The scope of psychoanalysis, 1921–1961.* New York: Basic Books.

Angyal, A. (1982). *Neurosis and treatment* (E. Hanfmann & R. M. Jones, Eds.). New York: Da Capo Press.

Arieti, S. (1979, January). New views on the psychodynamics of phobias. *American Journal of Psychotherapy, 33*(1), 82–95.

Auerbach, A. (1962). Attitudes of psychiatrists to the use of hypnosis. *Journal of the American Medical Association, 180*(11), 917–921.

Auerbach, C. (1985, Winter). What is a self?: A constructivist theory. *Psychotherapy, 22*(4), 743–746.

Axline, V. (1947). *Play therapy.* Boston: Houghton Mifflin.

Axline, V. (1964). Nondirective therapy. In M. R. Haworth (Ed.), *Child psychotherapy: Practice and theory.* New York: Basic Books.

Baker, R. A., & Patrick, B. S. (1987, Jan.). Hypnosis and memory: The effects of emotional arousal. *American Journal of Clinical Hypnosis, 29*(3), 177–184.

Balint, M. (1979). *The basic fault: Therapeutic aspects of regression.* New York: Brunner/Mazel.

Barber, J. (1980, July). Hypnosis and the unhypnotizable. *The American Journal of Clinical Hypnosis, 23*(1), 4–9.

Barnes, M. & Berke, J. (1971). *Mary Barnes.* New York: Ballentine.

Beckwith, L. (1985). Parent-Child interaction and social-emotional development. In C. C. Brown & A. W. Gottfried (Eds.). *Play interactions: The role of toys and parental involvement in children's development.* Johnson & Johnson.

Benedek, T. (1959). Parenthood as a developmental phase. *Journal of the American Psychoanalytic Association, 7*,(1–4), 389–417.

Bower, G. (1981). Mood and memory. *American Psychologist, 36*(2), 129–148.

Boyer, L. B. (1979). Countertransference with the severely regressed. In L. Epstein & A. Feiner (Eds.), *Countertransference*. New York: Jason Aronson, 347–374.

Brown, A. F. (1901). *The lonesomest doll*. Boston: Houghton Mifflin.

Brown, D. P. & Fromm, E. (1986). *Hypnotherapy and hypnoanalysis*. Hillsdale, NJ: Lawrence Erlbaum.

Brown, J. J. (1984, Spring). The response to self development: On the necessity of parallel development in analyst and patient. *Psychoanalytic Review, 71*(1), 103–121.

Brown, S. & Beletsis, S. (1986, January). The development of family transference in groups for the adult children of alcoholics. *International Journal of Group Psychotherapy, 36*(1), 97–114.

Carpenter, G., Meece, J., Stechler, O., & Friedman, S. (1978). Differential visual behavior to human and humanoid faces in early infancy. *Merrill Palmer Quarterly, 16*, 91–107.

Carroll, L. (1946). *Through the looking-glass*. New York: Random House.

Chambless, D. L. (1982). Characteristics of agoraphobics. In D. L. Chambless and A. J. Goldstein (Eds.). *Agoraphobia: Multiple perspectives on theory and treatment*. New York: Wiley, 1–18.

Clarke, A. M. & Clarke, A. D. B. (1976). *Early experience: Myth and evidence*. London: Open Books.

Diamond, M. J. (1980). The client as hypnotist: Furthering hypnotherapeutic change. *International Journal of Clinical and Experimental Hypnosis, 28*, 197–207.

Diamond, M. J. (1984, July). It takes two to tango: Some thoughts on the neglected importance of the hypnotist in an interactive hypnotherapeutic relationship. *American Journal of Clinical Hypnosis, 27*(1), 3–13.

Dowd, E. T. & Healy, J. M. (1986). *Case Studies in Hypnotherapy*. New York: Guilford.

Eastman, P. D. (1960). *Are you my mother?* New York: Beginner Books (Random House).

Ellis, M. J. (1973). *Why people play*. Englewood Cliffs, NJ: Prentice-Hall.

Emde, R. N., Gaensbauer, T. J., & Harmon, R. J. (1976). *Emotional expression in infancy: A biobehavioral study*. New York: International Universities Press.

Erickson, M. H. (1986). *Mind-body communication in hypnosis*, E. L. Rossi & M. O. Ryan (Eds.). New York: Irvington.

Erickson, M. H., Hershman, S., & Secter, I. I. (1981). *The practical application of medical and dental hypnosis*. Chicago: Seminars on Hypnosis.

Erickson, M. H., and Kubie, L. S. (1941). The successful treatment of a case of acute hysterical depression by a return under hypnosis to a critical phase of childhood. *Psychoanalytic Quarterly, 10*, 592–609.

Erickson, M. H., Rossi, E. L., & Rossi, S. I. (1976). *Hypnotic realities*. New York: Irvington.

Erickson, M. H. & Rossi, E. (1979). *Hypnotherapy: An exploratory casebook*. New York: Irvington.

Erickson, M. H., & Rossi, E. L. (1981). *Experiencing hypnosis*. New York: Irvington.

Erikson, E. H. (1951). Sex differences in the play configurations of preadolescents. *American Journal of Orthopsychiatry, 21*, 667–692.

Erikson, E. H. (1964). Toys and reasons. In M. R. Haworth (Ed.), *Child psychotherapy: Practice and theory*. New York: Basic Books, 3–11.

Erikson, E. H. (1968). *Identity, youth and crisis*. New York: Norton.

Evans, F. J., and Thorn, W. A. F. (1963). Source amnesia after hypnosis. *American psychologist, 18*, 393, Abstract.

Fagan, J. & McMahon, P. (1984, January). Incipient multiple personality in children. *The Journal of Nervous and Mental Disease, 172*(1), 26–36.

Fenichel, O. (1945). *The psychoanalytic theory of neurosis*. New York: Norton.

Ferenczi, S. (1956). Stages in the development of reality. In *Sex in psycho-analysis*. New York: Dover, 181–203.

Ferenczi, S. (1980a). Child-analysis in the analysis of adults. In M. Balint (Ed.), *Final contributions to the problems and methods of psycho-analysis*. New York: Brunner/Mazel, 126–142.

Ferenczi, S. (1980b). *Final contributions to the problems and methods of psycho-analysis*. New York: Brunner/Mazel.

Ferenczi, S. (1980c). Stages in the development of the sense of reality. In Ernest Jones (Trans.), *First contributions to psycho-analysis*. New York: Brunner/Mazel, 213–239.

French, T. M. (1961). Introduction to F. Alexander, *The scope of psychoanalysis, 1921–1961*. New York: Basic Books, viii.

Freud, A. (1963). Regression as a principle in mental development. *Bulletin of the Menninger Clinic. 27*, 126–139.

Freud, A. (1964). *The psychoanalytical treatment of children*. New York: Schocken Books.

Freud, S. (1897). Draft M. Notes II, Extract from the Fliess Papers. In J. Strachey (Trans. & Ed.), *The standard edition of the complete psychological works of Sigmund Freud* (Vol. 1). New York: Norton.

Freud, S. (1900). The interpretation of dreams. In J. Strachey (Trans. & Ed.), *The standard edition of the complete psycho-*

logical works of Sigmund Freud (Vol. 3, 4, and 5). New York: Norton.

Freud, S. (1905). On psychotherapy. In J. Strachey (Trans. & Ed.), *The standard edition of the complete psychological works of Sigmund Freud* (Vol. 7). New York: Norton.

Freud, S. (1911–13). The disposition to obsessional neurosis. In J. Strachey (Trans. & Ed.), *The standard edition of the complete psychological works of Sigmund Freud* (Vol. 12). New York: Norton.

Freud, S. (1913). On beginning the treatment. In J. Strachey (Trans. & Ed.), *The standard edition of the complete psychological works of Sigmund Freud* (Vol. 12). New York: Norton.

Freud, S. (1916–17). Introductory lectures on psychoanalysis. In J. Strachey (Trans. & Ed.), *The standard edition of the complete psychological works of Sigmund Freud* (Vol. 16). New York: Norton.

Freud, S. (1921). Group psychology and the analysis of the ego. In J. Strachey (Trans. & Ed.), *The standard edition of the complete psychological works of Sigmund Freud* (Vol. 18). New York: Norton.

Freud, S. (1925). An autobiographical study. In J. Strachey (Trans. & Ed.), *The standard edition of the complete psychological works of Sigmund Freud* (Vol. 20). New York: Norton.

Freud, S. (1926). Inhibitions, symptons, and anxiety. In J. Strachey (Trans. & Ed.), *The standard edition of the complete psychological works of Sigmund Freud* (Vol. 20). New York: Norton.

Freud, Sigmund. (1930). Civilization and its discontents. In J. Strachey (Trans. & Ed.), *The standard edition of the complete psychological works of Sigmund Freud* (Vol. 21). New York: Norton.

Freud, S. (1939). Moses and monotheism. In J. Strachey (Trans. & Ed.), *The standard edition of the complete psychological works of Sigmund Freud* (Vol. 23). New York: Norton.

Fromm, E. (1968). Transference and countertransference in hypnoanalysis. *The International Journal of Clinical and Experimental Hypnosis, 16*(2), 77–84.

Fromm, E. (1980, Winter). Values in hypnotherapy. *Psychotherapy: Theory, Research and Practice, 17*(4), 425–430.

Gardner, G. G. & Olness, K. (1981). *Hypnosis and hypnotherapy with children.* Orlando: Grune & Stratton.

Garvey, C. (1977). *Play.* Cambridge: Harvard University Press.

Gill, M. & Brenman, M. (1943). Treatment of a case of anxiety hysteria by a hypnotic technique employing psychoanalytic principles. *Bulletin of the Menninger Clinic, I*, 163–171.

Gill, M. & Brenman, M. (1959). *Hypnosis and related states: Psychoanalytic studies in regression.* New York: International Universities Press.

Gottfried, A. W. (1985). Introduction. In C. C. Brown & A. W. Gottfried (Eds.), *Play interactions: The role of toys and parental involvement in children's development.* Johnson and Johnson.

Greenacre, P. (1957). The childhood of the artist. In R. S. Eissler, A. Freud, H. Hartmann, M. Kris, & S. Lustman (Eds.), *The psychoanalytic study of the child* (Vol. 12). New York: International Universities Press.

Greenbaum, T. (1978). The 'analyzing instrument' and the 'transitional object.' In Grolnick, S. & Barkin, L. (Eds.) (in collaboration with W. Muensterberger). *Between reality and fantasy: Transitional objects and phenomena.* New York: Jason Aronson, 193–209.

Guntrip, H. (1969). *Schizoid phenomena, object relations and the self.* New York: International Universities Press.

Hafner, R. J. (1982). The marital context of agoraphobic syndrome. In D. L. Chambless & A. J. Goldstein (Eds.), *Agoraphobia: Multiple perspectives on theory and treatment.* New York: Wiley, 77–117.

Haworth, M. R. & Keller, J. (1964). The use of food in therapy. In M. R. Haworth (Ed.), *Child psychotherapy: Practice and theory.* New York: Basic Books, 330–338.

Hilgard, E. R. (1965). *Hypnotic susceptibility.* New York: Harcourt Brace Jovanovich.

Hilgard, E. R. (1966, April). Posthypnotic amnesia: Experiments and theory. *The International Journal of Clinical and Experimental Hypnosis, 14*(2), 104–111.

Hilgard, E. R. (1977). *Divided consciousness: Multiple controls in human thought and action.* New York: Wiley.

Irwin, E. C. (1963). The diagnosis and therapeutic use of pretend play. In C. E. Shaeffer (Ed.), *Handbook of play therapy.* New York: Wiley, 148–173.

Jacobson, E. (1938). *Progressive relaxation.* Chicago: University of Chicago Press.

Johnson, S. M. (1985). *Characterological transformation: The hard work miracle.* New York: Norton.

Judd, F. K., Burrows, G. D., & Dennerstein, L. (1986). Clinicians' perceptions of the adverse effects of hypnosis: A preliminary survey. *Australian Journal of Clinical and Experimental Hypnosis, 14*(1), 49–60.

Kagan, J. (1981). *The second year.* Cambridge: Harvard University Press.

Kagan, J. Kearsley, R. B., & Zelazo, P. R. (1980). *Infancy: Its place in human development.* Cambridge: Harvard University Press.

Kaplan, H. I. & Sadock, B. J. (1985). *Modern synopsis of comprehensive textbook of psychiatry/IV.* Baltimore: Williams & Wilkins.

Kaplun, D. & Reich, R. (1976, July). The murdered child and his killers. *American Journal of Psychiatry, 133*(7), 809–813.

Katz, N. W. (1985). The hypnotic lifestyle: Integrating hypnosis into everyday life. In J. K. Zeig (Ed.), *Ericksonian psychotherapy: Vol. I: Structures.* New York: Brunner/Mazel, 305–313.

Kernberg, O. (1985). Melanie Klein. In Kaplan, H. I. & Sadock, B. J. (Eds.), Theories of personality and psychopathology: Other schools. *Modern synopsis of comprehensive textbook of psychiatry/IV.* Baltimore: Williams & Wilkins.

Kestenberg, J. S. (1978). Transsensus – outgoingness and Winnicott's intermediate zone. In S. A. Grolnick & L. Barkin, (Eds.). *Between reality and fantasy: Transitional objects and phenomena.* New York: Jason Aronson.

Klein, M. (1975). *The psycho-analysis of children* (A. Strachey, Trans.) (Revised in collaboration with A. Strachey by H. A. Thorner). New York: The Free Press.

Kluft, R. (1985, April). Hypnotherapy of childhood multiple personality disorder. *American Journal of Clinical Hypnosis, 27*(4), 201–210.

Kluft, R. P. (1982, April). Varieties of hypnotic interventions in the treatment of multiple personality. *The American Journal of Clinical Hypnosis. 24*(4), 230–240.

Kohut, H. (1959). Introspection, empathy, and psychoanalysis. *Journal of the American Psychoanalytic Association, 7,* 459–483.

Kohut, H. (1984). *How does analysis cure?* Chicago: University of Chicago Press.

Kris, E. (1952). *Psychoanalytic explorations in art.* New York: International Universities Press.

Kubie, L. S. & Margolin, S. (1944, March). The process of hypnotism and the nature of the hypnotic state. *American Journal of Psychiatry, 100,* 611–622.

Laing, R. D. (1985, December 11). *Theoretical and practical aspects of psychotherapy.* Workshop delivered at the Evolution of Psychotherapy Conference, Phoenix, Arizona.

Lamb, C. S. (1985, October). Hypnotically-induced deconditioning: Reconstruction of memories in the treatment of phobias. *American Journal of Clinical Hypnosis 28*(2), 56–62.

Lankton, S. R. & Lankton, C. H. (1983). *The answer within: A clinical framework of Eriksonian hypnotherapy.* New York: Brunner/Mazel.

Lebo, D. (1952). The relationship to response categories in play therapy to chronological age. *Journal of Child Psychiatry, 2,* 330–336.

Lebo, D. (1956). Age and suitability for nondirective play therapy. *The Journal of Genetic Psychology, 89,* 232–238.

Levin, P. (1974). *Becoming the way we are.* Washington: Directed Media.

Lewis, L. (1985, Feb. 3). In on the game. *New York Times Magazine,* 70.

Lindner, H. (1960). The shared neurosis: Hypnotist and subject. *International Journal of Clinical and Experimental Hypnosis, 8,* 61–70.

Loewald, H. W. (1960). On the therapeutic action of psycho-analysis. *International Journal of Psycho-Analysis. 41,* 16–33.

Loftus, E. F. & Loftus, G. R. (1980, May). On the permanence of stored information in the human brain. *American Psychologist. 35*(5), 409–420.

Longman dictionary of psychology and psychiatry (1984). (R. M. Goldenson, Ed.). New York: Longman.

MacFarlane, J. (1975). Olfaction in the development of social preference in the human neonate. Ciba Foundation Symposium, *33, Parent-Infant interaction.* Amsterdam: Elsevier.

Mahler, M. S. (1972). Rapprochement subphase of the separation-individuation process. *Psychoanalytic Quarterly, 41,* 487–506.

Mahler, M. S., Pine, F., & Bergman, P. (1975). *The psychological birth of the human infant.* New York: Basic Books.

Mann, E. and McDermott, Jr., J. F. (1983). Play therapy for victims of child abuse and neglect. In C. E. Shaeffer & K. J. O'Connor (Eds.), *Handbook of play therapy.* New York: Wiley, 283–307.

Masterson, J. F. (1976). *Psychotherapy of the borderline adult: A developmental approach.* New York: Brunner/Mazel.

Masterson, J. F. (1985). *Treatment of the borderline adolescent: A developmental approach.* New York: Brunner/Mazel.

Matthews, W. J. (1985). A cybernetic model of Ericksonian hypnotherapy: One hand draws the other. In S. R. Lankton (Ed.), *Elements and dimensions of an Ericksonian approach.* New York: Brunner/Mazel.

McDougall, J. (1979). Primitive communication and the use of countertransference. In L. Epstein & A. Feiner (Eds.), *Countertransference.* New York: Jason Aronson, 267–303.

Meissner, W. W. (1978). *The paranoid process.* New York: Jason Aronson.

Michels, R. (1985). Transference: An introduction. E. A. Schwaber

(Ed.), *The transference in psychotherapy: Clinical manage-ment.* New York: International Universities Press.

Miller, A. (1986, January). Hypnotherapy in a case of incest. *The International Journal of Clinical and Experimental Hypnosis, 34*(1), 13–28.

Mott, T. Jr. (1982, April). The role of hypnosis in psychotherapy. *The American Journal of Clinical and Experimental Hypnosis, 24*(4), 241–248.

Mott, T. Jr. (1987). Editorial: Adverse reactions in the use of hypnosis. *American Journal of Clinical Hypnosis, 29*(3), pp. 147–148.

Musetto, A. P. (1985) Treating agoraphobia: A multidimensional view. In P. A. Keller & L. G. Ritt (Eds.), *Innovations in clinical practice: A source book* (Vol. 4.) Florida: Professional Resource Exchange, 5–22.

Nachman, P. & Stern, D. (1984). Retrieval: A form of recall memory in prelinguistic infants. In J. D. Call, E. Galenson, & R. L. Tyson (Eds.). *Frontiers of Infant Psychiatry (Vol 2.).* New York: Basic Books, 95–100.

Nash, M. R., Drake, S. D., Wiley, S., Khalsa, S., & Lynn, S. J. (1986). Accuracy of recall by hypnotically age-regressed subjects. *Journal of Abnormal Psychology, 95*(3), 298–300.

Orne, M. T. (1959). The nature of hypnosis: Artifact and essence. *Journal of Abnormal Social Psychology. 58*, 277–279.

Orne, M. T. (1966, April). On the mechanism of posthypnotic amnesia. *The International Journal of Clinical and Experimental Hypnosis. 14*(2), 121–134.

Orne, M. T. (1979, Oct.). Use and misuse of hypnosis in court. *The International Journal of Clinical and Experimental Hypnosis. 27*(4), 311–341.

Paul, I. H. (1959). Studies in remembering. *Psychological Issues, 1* (Monograph 2), New York: International Universities Press.

Phillips, R. D. (1985, Winter). Whistling in the dark? A review of play therapy research. *Psychotherapy, 22*(4), 752–760.

Pine, F. (1986, July). On the development of the 'borderline-child-to-be.' *American Journal of Orthopsychiatry, 56*(3), 450–457.

Pratt, G. J., Wood, D. P. & Alman, B. M. (1984). *A clinical hypnosis primer.* La Jolla: Psychology & Consulting Associates Press.

Racker, H. (1968). *Transference and counter-transference.* New York: International Universities Press.

Rossi, E. (1982, July). Hypnosis and ultradian cycles: A new state(s) theory of hypnosis? *American Journal of Clinical Hypnosis, 25*(1), 21–32.

Rossi, E. (1986). *The psychobiology of mind-body healing.* New York: Norton.

Rubin, K. H. (1985). Play, peer interaction, and social development.

In C. C. Brown & A. W. Gottfried (Eds.), *Play interactions.* Johnson & Johnson, 88–96.

Rutter, M. (1979). Separation experiences: A new look at an old topic. *The Journal of Pediatrics, 95*(1), 147–154.

Sacerdote, P. (1977). *Induced dreams.* New York: Theo. Gaus, Ltd.

Sachs, R. G. and Braun, B. G. (1986). The use of sand worlds with the MPD patient. In *Dissociative disorders: Proceedings of the third international conference on multiple personality/ dissociative states* (B. G. Braun Ed.). Chicago: Rush University.

Salzman, L. (1980). *Treatment of the obsessive personality.* New York: Jason Aronson.

Sands, S. (1986, August). The use of hypnosis in establishing a holding environment to facilitate affect tolerance and integration in impulsive patients. *Psychiatry, 49*(1), 218–230.

Scagnelli-Jobsis, J. (1982, July). Hypnosis with psychotic patients: A review of the literature and presentation of a theoretical framework. *American Journal of Clinical Hypnosis, 25*(1), 33–45.

Sechehaye, M. (1951a). *Autobiography of a schizophrenic girl,* New York: Grune and Stratton.

Sechehaye, M. (1951b). *Symbolic realization.* New York: International Universities Press.

Shapiro, M. K. (1977). The psychology of adult learning: The role of symbolism in the process of human being. Unpublished doctoral dissertation, Harvard Graduate School of Education, Cambridge.

Silverman, L. H., & Weinberger, J. (1985, December). Mommy and I are one. *American Psychologist, 40*(12), 1296–1308.

Silverman, P. S., & Retzlaff, P. D. (1986). Cognitive stage regression through hypnosis: Are earlier cognitive stages retrievable? *The International Journal of Clinical and Experimental Hypnosis, 34*(3), 192–204.

Smith, A. H. (1981, Spring). Object relations theory and family systems. *Psychotherapy: Theory, research and practice, 18*(1), 54–67.

Spiegel, D., Frischholz, E. J., Maruffi, B., & Spiegel, H. (1981). Hypnotic responsivity and the treatment of flying phobia. *American Journal of Clinical Hypnosis, 23,* 239–247.

Spiegel, H. (1972) An eye roll test for hypnotizability. *American Journal of Clinical Hypnosis, 15*(25), pp. 25–28.

Stedman's medical dictionary. (1982). (24th ed.). Baltimore: Williams & Wilkins.

Stern, D. (1985). *The interpersonal world of the infant.* New York: Basic Books.

Stone, L. (1961). *The psychoanalytic situation.* New York: International Universities Press.

Stone, M. H. (1980). *The borderline syndromes.* New York: McGraw-Hill.

Strachey, J. (1966). Freud's use of the concept of regression. In J. Strachey (Trans. & Ed.), *The Standard edition of the complete psychological works of Sigmund Freud* (Vol. 1). New York: Norton.

Stricherz, M. (1986). Hypnotic reparenting. In E. T. Dowd & J. M. Healy (Eds.), *Case studies in hypnotherapy.* New York: Guilford.

Sullivan, H. S. (1953). *The interpersonal theory of psychiatry.* (H. S. Perry & M. L. Gawel, Eds.). New York: Norton.

Terr, L. C. (1983). Play therapy and psychic trauma. In C. E. Shaeffer & K. J. O'Connor (Eds.), *Handbook of play therapy.* New York: Wiley, 308–316.

Watkins, H. H. (1980). The silent abreaction. *International Journal of Clinical and Experimental Hypnosis, 28,* 101–113.

Watkins, J. G. (1971). The affect bridge: A hypnoanalytic technique. *The International Journal of Clinical and Experimental Hypnosis, 19*(1), 21–27.

Watkins, J. G. (1984, April). The Bianchi (L.A. Hillside Strangler) case: Sociopath or multiple personality? *The International Journal of Clinical and Experimental Hypnosis, 32*(2), 67–101.

Weekes, C. (1972). *Peace from nervous suffering.* New York: Hawthorn Books.

Weiner, M. F. (1986). *Practical psychotherapy.* New York: Brunner/Mazel.

Weitzenhoffer, A. M. (1957). *General techniques of hypnotism.* New York: Grune & Stratton.

West, L. J., & Deckert G. H. (1965, April 5). Dangers of hypnosis. *Journal of the American Medical Association, 192* (11), 95–98.

Wester, W. C. II, & Smith, A. H. Jr. (1984). *Clinical hypnosis: A multidisciplinary approach.* Philadelphia: J. G. Lippincott.

Williams, J. A. (1985, July). Indirect hypnotic therapy of nyctophobia: a case report. *American Journal of Clinical Hypnosis, 28*(1), 10–15.

Winnicott, D. W. (1958a). Metaphysical and clinical aspects of regression within the psychoanalytic set-up. In *Collected papers: Through paediatrics to psycho-analysis.* London: Tavistock, 278–294.

Winnicott, D. W. (1958b). Birth memories, birth trauma, and anxiety. In *Collected papers: Through paediatrics to psycho-analysis.* London: Tavistock 174–193.

Winnicott, D. W. (1958c). Metapsychological and clinical aspects of regression within the psychoanalytical set-up. *Collected papers: Through paediatrics to psycho-analysis.* London: Tavistock, 278–294.

Winnicott, D. W. (1958d). Primitive emotional development. In *Collected papers: Through paediatrics to psycho-analysis.* London: Tavistock, 145–156.

Winnicott, D. W. (1958e). Anxiety associated with insecurity. In *Collected papers: Through paediatrics to psycho-analysis.* London: Tavistock, 97–100.

Winnicott, D. W. (1958f). Clinical varieties of transference. In *Collected papers: Through paediatrics to psycho-analysis.* London: Tavistock, 295–299.

Winnicott, D. W. (1958g). Primitive emotional development. In *Collected papers: Through paediatrics to psycho-analysis.* London: Tavistock, 45–156.

Winnicott, D. W. (1958h). Hate in the countertransference. In *Collected papers: Through paediatrics to psycho-analysis.* London: Tavistock, 194–203.

Winnicott, D. W. (1958i). Transitional objects and transitional phenomena. In *Collected papers: Through paediatrics to psycho-analysis.* London: Tavistock, 229–242.

Winnicott, D. W. (1958j). Mind and its relation to the psyche-soma. In *Collected papers: Through paediatrics to psycho-analysis.* London: Tavistock, 243–254.

Winnicott, D. W. (1965a). Dependence in infant-care, in child care, and in the psychoanalytic setting. In *The maturational processes and the facilitating environment.* New York: International Universities Press, 249–259.

Winnicott, D. W. (1965b). Psychotherapy of character disorders. In *The maturational processes and the facilitating environment.* New York: International Universities Press, 203–216.

Winnicott, D. W. (1965c). The development of the capacity for concern. In *The maturational processes and the facilitating environment.* New York: International Universities Press, 73–82.

Winnicott, D. W. (1965d). Ego integration in child development. In *The maturational processes and the facilitating environment.* New York: International Universities Press, 56–63.

Winnicott, D. W. (1986a). Living creatively. In C. Winnicott, R. Shepherd, & M. Davis (Eds.), *Home is where we start from.* New York: Norton, 39–54.

Winnicott, D. W. (1986b). Children learning. In C. Winnicott, R. Shepherd, and M. Davis (Eds.), *Home is where we start from.* New York: Norton, 142–149.

Wolf, E. S. (1979). Countertransference in disorders of the self. In

L. Epstein & A. H. Feiner (Eds.), *Countertransference*. New York: Jason Aronson.

Zeig, J. K. (Ed.). (1982). *Ericksonian approaches to hypnosis and psychotherapy*. New York: Brunner/Mazel.

Zeig, J. K. (Ed.). (1985a). *Ericksonian psychotherapy: Vol. I: Structures*. New York: Brunner/Mazel.

Zeig, J. K. (Ed.). (1985b). *Ericksonian psychotherapy: Vol. II: Clinical applications*. New York: Brunner/Mazel.

Zeig, J. K. (Ed.). (1985c). *Experiencing Erickson*. New York: Brunner/Mazel.

Zilbergeld, B. (1986). Choosing inductions. In B. Zilbergeld, M. G. Edelstien & D. L. Araoz (Eds.). *Hypnosis: questions and answers*. New York: Norton.

INDEX

INDEX OF CASES

GENERAL INDEX